The Immaculate Conception

in the Life of the Church

D1347589

The Immaculate Conception in the Life of the Church

Essays from the International Mariological Symposium in Honor of the 150th Anniversary of the Proclamation of the Dogma of the Immaculate Conception

Donald H. Calloway, M.I.C.
Editor

MARIAN PRESS
STOCKBRIDGE MA 01263

John Paul II Institute of Divine Mercy
An Imprint of Marian Press
2004

Nihil Obstat:
Rev. Richard J. Drabik, M.I.C.
Provincial Censor
March 25, 2004

Imprimi Potest:
Very Rev. Walter M. Dziordz, M.I.C., D. Min.
Provincial Superior
March 25, 2004

Library of Congress Catalog Number: 2004103367

ISBN: 1-932773-93-2

Editor: *Donald H. Calloway, M.I.C.*
Proofreader: *David Came*
Typesetting: *Marina Batiuk*
Cover Design: *William Sosa*

Special thanks: *Grace Mercado, Lucia D'Annunzio, Dr. Erlinda De La Pena, Elena Riechman, Anne & James Drisler, Immaculate Conception Parish (Clarksburg, West Virginia)*

Front Cover: The picture of the Immaculate Virgin Mary, commissioned by the Marians and painted by Franciszek Smuglewicz (1745-1807), was placed in St. Vitus Church in Rome in December of 1781. The church, along with the adjoining monastery, was the property of the Marians at that time.

Published by:
John Paul II Institute of Divine Mercy
An imprint of *Marian Press*

Marians of the Immaculate Conception
Stockbridge, Massachusetts 01262

TABLE OF CONTENTS

SUPERIOR GENERALIS
CONGREGATIONIS CC. MARIANORUM
AB IMMACULATA CONCEPTIONE B. V. M.

Via Corsica, 1
00198 Roma (ITALIA)

Tel. (06) 853.703.1;
853.703.34
Fax (06)853.703.34

February 19, 2004

Rev. Fr. Donald Calloway, M.I.C.
Marians of the Immaculate Conception
4 Prospect Hill Road, Eden Hill
Stockbridge, MA 01262

Dear Father Donald:

I want to thank you for the invitaion to participate in the Symposium commemorating the 150th Anniversary of the Definition of the Dogma of the Immaculate Conception of the Most Blessed Virgin Mary.

For our Congregation, and for the whole Church, this anniversary is a joyful moment. Mary's Immaculate Conception is, as our Constitutions (n. 6) proclaim, the "sign, strength and joy" of our religious vocation. "By this mystery, Mary urges us to trust in the unlimited fruitfulness of the work of redemption, to avoid all sin, to hold in highest esteem purity of heart, to imbue life fully with divine grace and charity, and to so upbuild the Church in unity 'that it be holy and immaculate.' " Hence, it is not only a privilege of the Blessed Virgin Mary which we contemplate and celebrate in this Dogma, it is a belief to be proclaimed and lived in our daily lives. The conferences and discussions that are planned for this Symposium are an excellent manner to enter more deeply into the meaning of this mystery and to make it a part of our daily Christian lives.

To you and to Mr. Robert Stackpole, S.T.D., the Director of the John Paul II Institute of the Divine Mercy, and to all those who assisted you, I and my Council exend our thanks for organizing this Symposium. I also extend my greetings and thanks to those who have agreed to speak at this gathering, and to all those who are in attendance. Due to other duties, I regret that I cannot be present with you in person. Nevertheless, please know that we at the Generalate will be with you in spirit.

Through the intercession of the Immaculate Virgin Mary, may God bless your gathering and make it spiritually fruitful!

Yours in Christ,

Fr. Mark T. Garrow, mic

Very Rev. Mark T. Garrow, M.I.C.
Superior General

PREFACE

The essays contained in this volume are the fruit of the International Mariological Symposium commemorating the 150th anniversary of the proclamation of the Dogma of the Immaculate Conception (1854-2004). The event itself took place at the John Paul II Cultural Center in Washington, D.C. from February 20-21, 2004. The Symposium was sponsored by the Congregation of Marians of the Immaculate Conception, and organized by the John Paul II Institute of Divine Mercy, which is the academic branch of the St. Stanislaus Kostka Province of the Marian community.

The inspiration for conducting such a symposium, and subsequent book, comes from the expressed desire of Pope John Paul II, made in October of 2002, that in order to bring this great mystery of our faith, the Immaculate Conception, to the people and cultures of our time, there should be in-depth studies done on the mystery of the Immaculate Conception during the 150th anniversary year. It is for this reason that the Congregation of Marians of the Immaculate Conception, founded in 1673 by the Venerable Servant of God Stanislaus Papczynski as the first men's community in the history of the Church to bear the privilege of the Immaculate Conception of Mary in its title, began preparations for holding various symposia and conferences throughout their worldwide Congregation.

The St. Stanislaus Kostka Province, based in Stockbridge, Massachusetts, brought together some of the most notable scholars in the English-speaking world in order to offer to God's people an International Mariological Symposium rich both in theological orthodoxy (*fides quaerens intellectum*) and filial devotion (theology on our knees).

It is rare indeed that internationally known scholars are able to collectively gather at one place. However, for the honor of Our Lady, the Marians were able to bring together representatives from some of the most "cutting edge" areas in current theology: Dr. Robert A. Stackpole (Divine Mercy); Dr. Mary Shivanandan and Sr. M. Timothy Prokes, F.S.E. (Theological Anthropology & Theology of the Body); Dr. Mark I. Miravalle and Fr. Peter Damian M. Fehlner, F.I. (Marian Coredemption & Mediation of All Graces). With such erudite and internationally known scholars as these, it is hoped that these academic essays, published in the order in which they were presented at the symposium, will leave a living legacy in honor of the Immaculate Conception. *De Maria Numquam Satis*!

Fr. Donald H. Calloway, M.I.C.

Editor

THE IMMACULATE CONCEPTION
IN CATHOLIC APOLOGETICS

Robert A. Stackpole, S.T.D.

Imagine that we could go back in time to the greatest of all the apostles – St. Peter, St. John, and St. Paul – and refer to them all our doctrinal questions and disputes. Suppose we had all three apostles on the same "Doctrinal Commission;" each one would bring to that commission their own specific concerns.

First, there would be St. Peter, the one whom Christ named the "Rock," of His Church: the only one to whom Jesus gave the "keys" of the Kingdom, and whom He appointed to be shepherd of His whole flock. The continuing ministry of Peter in the Church in the See of Rome is seen by Catholics the world over as the *rock of the Church's unity* and the *trustworthy reference point* of the authentic Catholic faith.

Secondly, there would be St. John, the "beloved disciple," the one who reclined on our Lord's breast at the Last Supper, and who alone among the apostles stood at the foot of His cross. The profound insights of St. John into the *deepest mysteries* of the Christian Faith have always been seen as the principal reference point for the theology of the Orthodox Churches of the East.

Third in our tribunal would be St. Paul: the apostle of the heart set free by divine grace. St. Paul is the one who taught us that all the Scriptures are "God-breathed" (that is, inspired by the Spirit), and St. Paul is the one who emphasized the *absolute gravity* of God's saving grace, bringing that gospel message throughout the world as the great apostle to the Gentiles. As a result, the Protestant Evangelical churches have always looked to St. Paul as their principal guide.

So, there is our triumvirate – St. Peter, St. John, and St. Paul – as the ultimate doctrinal commission: an apostolic ecumenical council!

Now, suppose we were to travel back in time to this tribunal, carrying in our hands a copy of the papal Bull *"Ineffabilis Deus"* of Bl. Pope Pius IX, the papal document of 1854 which defined as binding upon all Catholics the doctrine of the Immaculate Conception. Suppose we read the main section of that document to our tribunal, in order to seek their comments and approval. The document states:

> We declare, pronounce and define: the doctrine which holds that the most Blessed Virgin Mary was, from the first moment of her conception, by the singular grace and privilege of almighty God and in view of the merits of Christ Jesus the Savior of the human race, preserved immune from all stain of original sin, is revealed by God, and therefore, firmly and constantly to be believed by all the faithful.[1]

My best guess is that after reading this to our apostolic tribunal, there would be a lengthy and uncomfortable silence, finally broken by St. Peter with the words: "What in the world are you talking about?" It would not be the references to Mary that would baffle them at first; St. John would simply want to know what we meant by phrases such as "the merits" of Jesus Christ, or "original sin." And then we might try to explain by saying: "Well, by merits we mean that, since Jesus is the Second Person of the Blessed Trinity who assumed human nature in His incarnation, all His acts and sufferings in the flesh are of infinite value to His eternal Father . . .," etc. And then, of course, St. Paul would want to know what in the world we meant by Christ's "incarnation," and by phrases such as "the Second Person of the Blessed Trinity."

---

[1] Cf. *Catechism of the Catholic Church*, 491.

You see at once the problem. All of these phrases (the "merits" of Christ, "original sin," "incarnation," and "Blessed Trinity") do not occur in the apostolic writings. To be sure, the "ideas" were there from the beginning, and so it would not be too difficult to show how each of these doctrines is contained, at least implicitly if not explicitly, in the teachings of these same apostles. In short, the doctrine of Mary's Immaculate Conception presupposes a long history of the unfolding and clarification of these central doctrines of the apostolic Faith, and it is only after all of these other doctrines were fully developed that the Church could even begin to consider clearly the question of how God prepared Mary for her special vocation as Mother of the Savior.

The doctrine of the Immaculate Conception, therefore, is a classic case of what the Church calls the "development of doctrine" – indeed, it is a legitimate development based on other developments. This means that unless your audience already understands and accepts the Catholic doctrine of "development," it is going to be very hard to lead them to the truth of Mary's Immaculate Conception.

I.   The Development of Doctrine

In its "Dogmatic Constitution on Divine Revelation," the Second Vatican Council states:

> [The doctrinal] tradition, which comes from the apostles, develops in the Church, with the help of the Holy Spirit. For there is growth in the understanding of the realities and the words that have been handed down. This happens through contemplation and study made by believers, who treasure these things in their hearts (cf. Luke 2:19, 51), through the intimate understanding of spiritual things they experience, and through the preaching of those who have received through episcopal succession the sure gift of truth. For, as the centuries succeed one another, the church constantly moves forward toward the fullness of divine truth until the words of God reach their complete fulfillment in her.[2]

---

[2]Second Vatican Council, "Dogmatic Constitution on Divine Revelation," Section 8, in Walter Abbott, S.J., Editor, *The Documents of Vatican II* (London: Geoffrey Chapman, 1967), 116.

What the Vatican Council meant, of course, is that doctrine properly develops in the Church by the drawing out of what was contained in the apostolic Tradition from the beginning. A legitimate doctrinal development, therefore, cannot be an utterly *novel addition* to the apostolic Faith, nor can it contradict anything in the original apostolic Faith. Thus, what St. Jude calls the truth "once and for all delivered to the saints" (Jude 3) was certainly present in the Church, at least in "seed" form, right from the time of the apostles. The essence or substance of the apostolic Faith remains unchanged. It is only the *conscious, subjective grasp* of the mysteries of the Faith that can grow and develop over time. In short, there is an increase in *understanding* of the apostolic Faith down through the centuries, as the Holy Spirit guides the prayers, meditations, and cumulative reflections of the whole Body of Christ, and especially of the saints and the Magisterium.

Doctrinal understanding properly can be said to "develop" in the Church in two ways: first by *clarification of expression*, and second, by *elaboration of content.*

Simple clarification of expression occurred, for example, when the early Church fashioned the distinction between "person" (hypostasis) and nature (physis) so that she articulate more clearly the doctrines of the Incarnation (that Jesus is one person in two natures) and the Trinity (that God is three persons sharing one nature).

By elaboration of content, on the other hand, is meant the drawing out of the implications of what was substantially present from the beginning. Such "elaboration" can take place in at least two ways. First, *logically* (that is, when the Church draws out the logical implications of apostolic teaching). For example, the full doctrine of original sin may be said to be logically implicit in the story of the Fall in Genesis, and in St. Paul's epistle to the Romans. Another example: the doctrine of the "just war" elaborated in the seventeenth century by Suarez may be said to be logically implicit in the attitude of Christ to soldiers, of St. Paul to the use of the "sword" by rulers – and also in the prior elaboration of the doctrine of original sin.

Secondly, elaboration can happen *mystically* (that is, by the Church discerning, and coming to a consensus about, the deeper ramifications of covenanted images, metaphors, even visions and prophecies, passed down to us from the apostles). For example, the doctrine of the Eucharistic Sacrifice may be said to be prophetically foreshadowed in the words of Malachi (1:11) about the "pure" offering to the Lord that will one day be offered all over the world. Or another example: the basic principles of the monastic life may be said to involve the bringing together of several elements of Christ's teaching, and the example of Mary in consecrated virginity.

In short, whether the Church is merely clarifying its verbal expression of apostolic teaching, or unfolding logical and mystical implications of the content of that teaching, either way, the Church grows in her understanding of the original, apostolic witness, and of its wider ramifications for living out the Christian faith in the world.

Unfortunately, the Catholic view of the "development of doctrine," outlined above, has been partially rejected by our Eastern Orthodox brethren. Here is a portion of "The Reply of the Synod of Constantinople to Pope Leo XIII" in 1895, just after the Pope had called for the return of the Eastern Churches to full communion with the Apostolic See:

> It is manifest that the universal Church of God, which holds fast in its bosom unique, unadulterated and entire this salutary faith as a divine deposit, just as of old it was delivered and *unfolded* by the God-bearing Fathers moved by the Spirit, and formulated by them during the first nine centuries, is one and the same forever, and not manifold and varying with the process of time: *because the gospel truths are never susceptible to alteration or progress in the course of time, like the various philosophical systems*; 'for Jesus Christ is the same yesterday, and today, and forever.' Wherefore

also the holy Vincent [of Lerins] who was brought up on the milk of piety received from the Fathers in the monastery of Lerins in Gaul, and flourished about the middle of the fifth century, with great wisdom and orthodoxy characterizes the true catholicity of the Faith and of the Church saying 'In the Catholic Church we must especially take heed to hold that which has been believed everywhere, at all times, and by all. For this is truly and properly catholic, as the very force and meaning of the word signifies, which moreover comprehends almost everything universally. And this we shall do, if we walk following universality, antiquity, and content.' But as has been said before, *the western Church, from the tenth century onwards, has privily brought into herself through the papacy various and strange and heretical doctrines and innovations,* and so she has been torn away and removed far from the true and orthodox Church of Christ. How necessary it is, then, for you to come back and return to the ancient and universal doctrines of the Church . . ."[3]

Presumably the doctrine of the Immaculate Conception is one of those "strange innovations" fostered by the papacy that the Synod of Constantinople would find objectionable.

In any case, there are three major problems with this Orthodox rejection of any true "development" or "progress" of doctrine.

1). First of all, this statement by the Synod of Constantinople is self-contradictory: all doctrinal "progress" is rejected, and yet the ancient Fathers are said to have "unfolded" the truths of the Faith under the guidance of the Spirit. If we are to say that the Spirit guided the patristic Church to "unfold" many of the mysteries of the Faith, why do we not allow that the Holy Spirit can continue that "unfolding" process in the Middle Ages, the early modern era, and even today? And did not that patristic labor of "unfolding" of the Faith result in some "progress" in the Church's apprehension of it?

---

[3]*The Reply of the Orthodox Church to Roman Catholic overtures on Reunion: Being the Answer of the Great Church of Constantinople To A Papal Encyclical on Reunion*, section 24 (New York: Orthodox Christian Movement of St. John the Baptist, 1958), 25-27.

2). Secondly, in order to reject all doctrinal "progress," you have to hold that all the beliefs definitively professed by the ancient Church of the early centuries were explicitly held by ecumenical consensus right from the beginning, that is, from the very time of the apostles onward. There may have been clarification of the language in which the Faith was expressed, improved articulation, but there was no elaboration of content, no drawing out over time of the logical/mystical implications of the original deposit of Faith. Now, this is surely an exceedingly difficult position to hold in the light of historical research. For example, do we have any evidence at all for the direct invocation of the saints by the apostolic or sub-apostolic churches (i.e., the first and second generations of Christians)? Does the Church of the first two centuries clearly and explicitly confess the entire sinlessness of the Blessed Virgin Mary? Or the Eucharist as a propitiatory sacrifice? These doctrines may be logically/mystically implicit in the apostolic Scriptures and teaching Tradition, but it surely took the Church some time – in some cases centuries – to discern and fully appreciate those implications. Again, did the ancient Fathers arrive at any clarity or consensus as to what our Lord and His apostles really meant by His death as a "ransom" for many (Mk. 10:45, I Pet. 1:18-19)? Or take two doctrines dear to the hearts of our Orthodox brethren: what evidence is there to show that the apostles and the earliest Christians explicitly believed in an eternal progress of the redeemed soul after death, or in a distinction between the unknowable "essence" and "energies" of God? An Orthodox theologian may want to defend both of these doctrines, but it is surely only possible to do so if one can show that these doctrines were at first hidden, logically/mystically implicit in Scripture and apostolic Tradition, and only later drawn out into the clear daylight of conscious understanding through the meditations and reflections of the saints and the Fathers.

In his essay, "Doing Theology in an Eastern Orthodox Perspective," John Meyendorff explained that the Orthodox "would be reluctant to accept unreservedly the predominant Roman Catholic view about doctrinal development, as found, for instance, in John Henry Newman. In the Orthodox Church," he claims, "formal doctrinal definitions are concerned only with *essentials*, without which the whole New Testament vision of salvation would not stand. This was certainly the case for the dogmas of the seven ecumenical councils, including the decree of Nicea II (787), on the veneration of icons, which in fact is not so much a decree on religious art as an affirmation of the reality of the incarnation; that is to say, it is a statement that Christ was an historical person – visible, depictable, representable."[4]

A Catholic following in the footsteps of Newman, however, would say that the decree of Nicea II concerning holy icons is a clear instance of proper doctrinal "development." Nicea II did not define one of the "essentials" of the Faith; rather, it settled a disputed *implication* of those essentials: namely, the propriety of making and venerating holy images. It is exceedingly doubtful that Christians in the apostolic era venerated icons, although in the sub-apostolic era they began to paint them on the walls of the catacombs. This shows that by the Holy Spirit the earliest generations of Christians had an initial, intuitive appreciation of the connection between their incarnational faith and sacred art long before that connection was theologically articulated and defended by St. John Damascene, and applied to the actual veneration of icons. What Nicea II did was to reaffirm and ratify this proper "development." Thus, the implications of the incarnational faith of the apostles with regard to sacred art were gradually drawn out and lived by later generations of Christians, and finally defined and secured by the Magisterium in ecumenical council.

3). Finally, the rejection of all "progress" or "development" of doctrine by the Synod of Constantinople was really somewhat disingenuous. The synod appealed to the teachings of St. Vincent of Lerins to bolster its case. In the same work

---

[4]John Meyendorff, "Doing Theology in an Eastern Orthodox Perspective" in Daniel Clendenin, ed., *Eastern Orthodox Theology: A Contemporary Reader* (Grand Rapids: Paternoster Press, 2003), 90.

in which they quote St. Vincent, however, the saint goes on to say while the ancient Catholic Faith is certainly unchangeable in its essence, this does not preclude "progress" in "understanding" of the Faith (Commonitory, 23, 28):

> But perhaps someone is saying: 'Will there, then, be no progress of religion in the Church of Christ?' Certainly there is, and the greatest. For who is there so envious toward men and exceedingly hateful toward God that he would try to prohibit progress? But it is truly progress, and not a change of the faith. *What is meant by progress is that something is brought to an advancement within itself; by change, something is transformed from one thing into another. It is necessary, therefore, that understanding, knowledge, and wisdom grow and advance strongly and mightily as much in individuals as in a group, as much in one man as in the whole Church, and this gradually according to age and the times; and this must take place precisely within its own kind, that is, in the same teaching, in the same meaning, and in the same opinion.* The progress of religion in souls is like the growth of bodies, which, in the course of years, evolve and develop, but still remain what they were . . .

> For example: *our fathers of old sowed the seeds of the wheat of faith in this field which is the Church.* Certainly it were unjust and incongruous if we, their descendants, were to gather instead of the genuine truth of wheat, the noxious error of weeds. On the contrary, it is right and logically proper that there be no discrepancy between what is first and what is last, what we sow and what we reap, and that we reap from the wheat of instruction the fruit also of dogma. And thus, although in the course of time *something evolved from those first seeds*, and has now expanded under careful cultivation, nothing of the characteristics of the seeds is changed. Granted that *appearance, beauty, and distinction have been added, still the same nature of each kind remains.*[5]

Consider also the witness of St. Augustine, who taught that the Catholic Church truly progresses in its understanding of the Faith, especially under the threat posed by heresy (City of God, bk. XVI, c.2, n.1):

---

[5] St. Vincent of Lerins, "The Notebooks," 23.28, in William A. Jurgens, ed. *The Faith of the Early Fathers*, vol. III (Collegeville: Liturgical Press, 1979), 265.

> When astutely attacked by heretics, many truths concerning the
> Catholic Faith are considered by Catholics with greater diligence
> in order to protect them from such attacks, and they are likewise
> understood more clearly and preached with greater urgency, so
> that the question raised by the enemy becomes a means of
> progress in knowledge of the faith.

In this essay, therefore, I am going to argue that the doctrine of the Immaculate Conception is a true and legitimate development of doctrine: an unfolding of things hidden and implicit in the apostolic Faith. In this sense, the doctrine (as finally defined by the See of Peter) represents genuine "progress" in the Church in the "understanding" of that deposit of faith. I shall argue that the doctrine has its "seeds" in Scripture, and in an intuitive appreciation by the ancient saints and Fathers of the mystery of the Lord's dealings with the Blessed Virgin Mary. The solemn definition 150 years ago by Pius IX was merely the culmination of centuries of meditation, theological debate, and verbal refinement, a slow and gradual drawing up of this mystery from the deep well-springs of Scripture and ancient Tradition into the full light of day.

Finally, I will try to show how the characteristic concerns of Pauline and Johannine Christianity (discussed above), manifest in the Evangelical and Orthodox traditions respectively, are already implicit in this beautiful doctrine. The Immaculate Conception is not just an isolated "privilege" given to Mary; rather, it tells us something about the Church dear to the heart of the Orthodox East, and something about divine grace dear to the heart of the Evangelical West. Far from being an obstacle to ecumenism, therefore, I believe that Mary's Immaculate Conception, properly understood, will one day become a point of convergence. Indeed, as our Lord from His Cross entrusted all His beloved disciples to the motherly care of Mary (Jn. 19:25-27) how could she have any other role and office than to bring the family of her Son together again, in one heart and mind?

II.   Clarification of the Doctrine of The Immaculate Conception

Let us begin by clarifying exactly what the doctrine of Mary's Immaculate Conception really means. The *Catechism of the Catholic Church* sums it up for us:

Through the centuries the Church has become ever more aware that Mary, "full of grace" through God, was redeemed from the first moment of her conception. That is what the dogma of the Immaculate Conception confesses, as Pope Pius IX proclaimed in 1854:

> The most Blessed Virgin Mary was, from the first moment of her conception, by a singular grace and privilege of almighty God and by virtue of the merits of Jesus Christ, Savior of the human race, preserved immune from all stain of original sin.

> The "splendor of an entirely unique holiness" by which Mary is "enriched from the first instant of her conception" comes wholly from Christ: she is "redeemed, in a more exalted fashion, by reason of the merits of her Son."[6]

Notice not only what this teaching of the Magisterium says, but also what it does *not* say. It does not say that it was necessary for Mary to be sanctified in this way so that her Son Jesus could be preserved from the stain of original sin. Perhaps God could have preserved Jesus from the corruption of original sin in some other way. We do not know. The Magisterium does not speculate on this aspect of the matter, and such speculative issues play no part in magisterial teaching here.

Moreover, the Magisterium does not claim that Mary was preserved from all stain of original sin on the grounds that her parents, Joachim and Anne, were preserved from all lust, all concupiscence, in the conjugal act by which Mary was conceived. In fact, that conjugal act is not mentioned by the Magisterium at all, only the "moment" of Mary's concep-

---

[6] *Catechism*, no. 491-492.

tion; from the first instant of her existence she is said to be specially graced by God. Besides, the idea that the corruption of original sin is transmitted from generation to generation by the concupiscence involved in the conjugal act, while it may be an interesting speculation derived from St. Augustine, has never been endorsed by the Church. Hence, it plays no part at all in the definition of the mystery of the Immaculate Conception.

Finally, and most importantly, the Magisterium does not say that as a result of her Immaculate Conception, Mary did not need to be redeemed by Jesus Christ. Quite the opposite; the Catholic Church teaches that the grace of the Immaculate Conception was given to Mary "by virtue of the merits of Jesus Christ," and "she is redeemed in a more exalted fashion, by reason of the merits of her Son." Enshrined in magisterial teaching here is the idea of "Preservative Redemption" which comes from the Franciscan Bl. Duns Scotus in the fourteenth century: As Fr. Garrigou-Lagrange, O.P., once put it: "Even in human affairs we look on one as more of a savior if he wards off a blow than if he merely heals the wound it inflicts."[7] From Mary's soul, therefore, the Lord warded off the blow of original sin, rather than merely healing her later of its effects. Given that God exists beyond all time, and all times are present before Him, He has the power to apply the graces of Christ's redemptive work to people living at any time in human history, – and He did so for Mary, from the first moment of her existence.

My favorite explanation of this point comes from a beautiful little work of apologetics from the Philippines, written by Fr. Adolf Faroni, SDB, and entitled *Know and Defend What You Love.* Fr. Faroni writes:

> An objection to the Immaculate Conception of Mary claims that Mary cannot be Immaculate, otherwise she would not have been redeemed by Jesus. This would detract from the universality of the redemption of Jesus, the only mediator

---

[7] Reginald Garrigou-Lagrange, O.P., *The Mother of the Savior* (Rockford: TAN Books, 1993), 48.

between God and all men (I Tim. 2:5), in whom alone there is salvation (cf. Acts 4:12). Mary herself calls God her "Savior" (Lk. 1:47).

The objection shows a fundamental misconception that to be full of grace meant absence of redemption. On the contrary, it *implies* redemption because Mary's fullness of grace is the fruit of the saving death of Christ . . .

Mary has been redeemed like us, only in a more wonderful way, not by cure but by prevention. A doctor can save our life by curing sickness. But if he gives us a medicine that keeps us from getting sick, he saves us much better.[8]

According to Orthodox Archbishop John Maximovitch, however, in his book, *Mary the Birthgiver of God*, "[this teaching] makes God unmerciful and unjust, because if God could preserve Mary from sin and purify her before her birth, then why does He not purify other men before their birth?"[9] Similarly, we might ask: why does the Lord not appear to everyone in a burning bush, as He did to Moses, or strike all sinners blind with the light of Christ, as He did to St. Paul on the Damascus road? The answer, surely, is that *extraordinary graces are usually given to those to whom the Lord entrusts extraordinary responsibilities*. Mary was given the singular grace of an immaculate origin in order to prepare her for her singular vocation: the special responsibility of being the Mother of God incarnate.

III.   Seeds of the Doctrine in Holy Scripture

There are two passages in Holy Scripture where we can find what St. Vincent of Lerins might have called "the seeds" of the doctrine of the Immaculate Conception. The first is the angel Gabriel's salutation to the Blessed Virgin

---

[8] Fr. Adolf Faroni, SDB, *Know and Defend What You Love* (Makati City, Philippines: Don Bosco Press, no date given), 47.

[9] John Maximovitch, *The Orthodox Veneration of the Mother of God* (Platina, California: Saint Herman of Alaska Brotherhood, 1978), 45. [original title of the work].

Mary in Luke 1:28-30: "Hail, full of grace, the Lord is with you! . . . Do not be afraid, Mary, for you have found favor with God." The second passage is what is traditionally called the "protoevangelium" – the first prophetic hint of the gospel – in Genesis 3:15, in which the Lord, after declaring the punishment meted out to the serpent, finishes with the words:

> I will put enmity between you and the woman,
> and between your seed and her seed;
> he shall bruise your head,
> and you shall bruise his heel.

(a)   Luke 1:28

Let us look at the gospel passage first. No one would claim that St. Luke the evangelist consciously believed in Mary's Immaculate Conception. Nevertheless, he must have realized that Mary's soul was graced in a truly extraordinary way, for under the guidance of the Holy Spirit he was led to record (perhaps from the testimony of Mary herself: Luke 2:19, 51) the angel Gabriel's salutation to her as (in Greek): "Kecharitomene," "full of grace."

The first thing to notice is that the angel does not address Mary by name here; he does not say, "Hail Mary" (as we say in the Rosary), but, in effect, he gives her a new name. As the Catholic apologist David Armstrong points out, "it was as if the angel were addressing Abraham 'Hail, full of faith,' or Solomon 'Hail, full of wisdom' (characteristics for which they were particularly noteworthy)."[10] For the ancient Hebrews names signified the character, nature, and qualities of a person, or their role in God's plan of salvation (so Simon was renamed "Rock" because he was to be the rock of the Church, and Jesus' own name, chosen by God Himself, means "God is salvation"). The mystery of Mary is summed up in her new name, "full of grace."

Secondly, the word "kecharitomene" comes from the root word "charis" in Greek, a word which was translated as

---

[10] Dave Armstrong, *A Biblical Defense of Catholicism* (1st Books Library, 2001), 128.

"grace" by the King James Version 129 times (out of 150 total appearances. In *An Expository Dictionary of New Testament Words,* the Protestant scholar W. E. Vine had this to say about "kecharitomene":

> "Charitoo": akin to "charis," to endow with "charis," primarily signified to make graceful or gracious, and came to denote, in Hellenistic Greek, to cause to find favour, Luke 1:28, "highly favoured" (margin "endued with grace") . . . Grace implies more than favour; grace is a free gift, favour may be deserved or gained.[11]

Here Vine points to an important issue. Most Protestant Bible translations, and even some Catholic ones today translate "kecharitomene" as "Hail, o favored one," or (as in the King James) "Hail, thou that art highly favored." But "favor" has a somewhat different connotation from the root word "charis." For as Vine points out, "grace" (charis) usually implies a free gift, according to Scripture, whereas someone's "favor" can be earned or deserved. According to the Protestant scholar A. T. Robertson, the angel Gabriel's salutation implies a gratuitous gift. "Kecharitomene," Robertson claims, "means endowed with grace (charis), enriched with grace, as in Ephesians 1:6 . . . [the Latin] Vulgate [translation] 'gratia plena' is right, if it means 'full of grace which thou has *received.*'"[12]

This leads to a third point about the angelic salutation. A "favor" can be something external – an external honor or blessing of some kind – whereas "grace" (charis) in Scripture, and especially in the New Testament, is often connected to an *interior* gift of some kind. The context of this passage certainly suggests the latter interpretation. It is not clear that the angel is pointing to any external honors or temporal rewards. The "charis" that Mary receives is a free gift of God, and a hidden gift, wrought in secret.

Of course, one might say, that the free gift with which Mary will be "graced" is simply the Christ child. Mary will be graced in the sense that she is chosen to conceive in the hid-

---

[11] As quoted in Armstrong, 127.

[12] Ibid., 127-128.

denness of her womb the Savior of the world. However, the angel speaks of a gift that Mary had *already* received, even before the angel came to her! This is clear from the fact that "kecharitomene" is neither in the present nor the future tense; it is a perfect passive participle. In other words, the angel does not say to her "Hail, you who *will be* fully graced (that is, in the future, when you conceive in your womb and bring forth a son)," nor does the angel say "Hail, you who are *right now* fully graced, in my message to you declaring that you are the one chosen to be the Mother of the Savior." Rather, the angel says to her "Hail, you who have already been fully graced, in a completed way, in the past." Fr. Clement Englert, C.SS.R. builds on this exegetical point as follows:

> It is remarkable that the Greek used the perfect participle here. The perfect does not refer so much to time or tense in this case, but rather to the kind of action, namely perfected, fully completed. If the author had wished merely to indicate past time, he had the aorist participles at his disposal. And so the word "kecharitomene" does not mean here simply "having been graced," but rather, "completely graced, perfectly graced." The same feature of the perfect form in Greek syntax applies also to the imperative and the infinitive. It is therefore not just some abstruse exception . . . it is a regular feature of Greek syntax.[13]

It would follow that to be completely *graced* by God cannot involve just an external favor of some kind. To be completely graced must refer also to an *inner spiritual gift,* a gift that *completely* fills the soul from the very first moment of the soul's existence onward (otherwise, the grace would not be "complete"). In fact, that is precisely what the Catholic Church means by teaching that Mary was conceived without the wound of original sin: she received a plenitude of sanctifying grace, poured into her heart from the Holy Spirit right from the start. As the Catechism puts it: "Enriched from the instant of her conception with the splendor of an entirely unique holiness . . ."

Even if Fr. Englert has overstated the exigetical case here (not being a Biblical linguist myself, I am not fully qualified to

---

[13] Clement C. Englert, C.SS.R., *Catholics and Orthodox: Can They Unite?* (New York: Paulist Press, 1961), 71-72.

judge), nevertheless, there is one more remarkable feature of this angelic word "kecharitomene," which points toward this mystery. I am referring to the undeniable fact that *the angelic salutation to Mary is the only place in Holy Scripture where this word of address is used.* Mary alone in the Bible is called "kecharitomene." The principal author of Holy Scripture, the Holy Spirit, guided St. Luke to choose just this word, and no other, to sum up the mystery of Mary: a unique word in all of the Bible to point toward the mystery of a singular grace.

(b)   Genesis 3:15

Given that the New Testament is the fulfillment of promises from the Lord contained in the Old, we would rightly find it hard to believe that Mary could have received such an extraordinary grace if we did not find this mystery foreshadowed in some way in the Jewish Scriptures. In fact, according to the Catholic Church, that is precisely what we do find in the "protoevangelium" in Genesis, Chapter 3. An excellent discussion of this Biblical passage is given to us in Dr. Mark Miravalle's work, *Introduction to Mary*. Aside from a few marginal comments of my own, I intend to quote his analysis in full. Dr. Miravalle writes:

> In Genesis 3:15, after Adam and Eve committed Original Sin, God addresses Satan, who is represented by the serpent: "I will put enmity between you and the woman and between your seed and her seed; he shall crush your head, and you shall lie in wait for his heel." Since the "seed" of the woman is Jesus Christ, who is to crush Satan victoriously in the redemption, then "the woman" must in fact refer to Mary, Mother of the Redeemer. [I would add a further bit of evidence here: according to St. John's gospel, Jesus twice refers to His mother as "woman" – at the wedding feast in Cana (Jn. 2:4) and from the Cross (Jn. 19:26) – and this was either an insulting way to speak to His mother, or it was a reference to the "woman" of the protoevangelium, identifying Mary directly with the "woman" of Genesis 3:15; a connection made again in the Joannine literature in Revelation 12:1-5].

The word "enmity," which is rich in meaning in this passage, signifies "in opposition to." The enmity established between the "seed" of the woman, which is Jesus, and the "seed" of the serpent, which is sin, and all evil angels and humans, is an absolute and complete opposition, because there is absolute and complete opposition between Jesus and all evil. In other words, the seed of the woman and the seed of Satan have to be in complete and total opposition to each other as depicted in the term "enmity."

Further in the passage we see the identical, God-given opposition or enmity given and proclaimed by God between the woman, Mary, and the serpent, Satan. Mary is given the same absolute and perpetual opposition to Satan as Jesus possesses in relation to sin. It is for this reason that Mary could not have received a fallen nature as a result of Original Sin. Any participation in the effects of Original Sin would place the Mother of Jesus in at least partial participation with Satan and sin, thereby destroying the complete, God-given opposition as revealed in Genesis 3.

The opposition between Jesus and sin is paralleled by the opposition between the woman, Mary, and the serpent, Satan. Again, this tells us that Mary could not participate in the fallen nature because that would mean participating, at least partially, in the domain of sin, a reality to which God gave Mary complete opposition.[14]

I am not claiming here that the doctrine of the Immaculate Conception can be *proven* solely from Luke 1:28 and Gen 3:15 – at least, not apart from the added witness, and interpretive "lens" of ancient Tradition. Nevertheless these two Scripture passages do converge, pointing together toward the wonderful truth of Blessed Mary's "fullness of grace." They are the scriptural "seeds" (as St. Vincent might say) of the developed doctrine.

IV.   Seeds of the Doctrine in Early Tradition

The common teaching of the early Fathers of the Church was that, just as Jesus is explicitly called by St. Paul the Second Adam, the Head of redeemed humanity, so the Blessed Virgin Mary is, implicitly in Scripture, the Second Eve. As Eve, the

---

[14] Mark Miravalle, S.T.D., *Introduction to Mary* (Santa Barbara: Queenship, 1993), 37-38.

Mother of all the living, had ushered in the age of sin by suc-cumbing to the temptation of the fallen angel, the serpent, so Mary, the Mother of all the Redeemed, reversed Eve's sin by her obedience to the angel Gabriel at the Annunciation. In the mid-second century, for example, St. Justin Martyr wrote in his *Dialogue with Tryphon* (100):

> By what way the disobedience arising from the serpent had its beginning, by what way also it might have an undoing. For Eve, being a virgin and undefiled, conceiving the word that was from the serpent, brought forth disobedience and death; but the Virgin Mary, taking faith and joy, when the angel told her the good tid-ings, that the Spirit of the Lord should come upon her and the power of the Highest overshadow her, and therefore the Holy One that was born of her was the Son of God, answered "Be it unto me according to Thy word."[15]

We find a similar teaching in Tertullian of Carthage (De Carn. Christ. 17):

> What by that [female] sex had gone into perdition, by that same sex might be brought back to salvation. Eve had believed the ser-pent; Mary believed Gabriel; the fault which the one committed by believing, the other by believing has blotted out.[16]

Again, we find this same teaching echoed by St. Ireneus of Lyons in his great work *Against Heresy* (iii. 22. 34):

> Mary, having the predestined man, and being yet a virgin, being obedient, became both to herself and to the whole human race the cause of salvation . . . And so the knot of Eve's disobedience received its unloosing through the obedience of Mary; for what Eve, a virgin, bound by incredulity, that Mary, a virgin, unloosed by faith.[17]

And again, in the same work, St. Ireneus wrote (v. 19):

> As Eve by the speech of an angel was seduced so as to flee God, transgressing His word, so also Mary received the good tidings by

---

[15] As quoted in John Henry Newman, *Mary – the Second Eve* (Leominster, England: Fowler-Wright Books, 1977), 3.

[16] Ibid., 3.

[17] Ibid., 4.

means of the angel's speech, so as to bear God within her, being obedient to His word. And, though the one had disobeyed God, yet the other was drawn to obey God; that of the Virgin Eve the Virgin Mary might become the advocate. And as by a virgin the human race had been bound by death, by a virgin it is saved, the balance being preserved, a virgin's disobedience by a virgin's obedience.[18]

This doctrine of Mary as essentially the "Second Eve" occurs also in numerous places in the writings of the post-Nicene Fathers. St. Epiphanius of Cyprus (d. 400), for example, writes: "Eve became a cause of death to men . . . and Mary a cause of life" (Haer. 78. 18); St. Jerome's slogan was "Death by Eve; life by Mary" (Ep. 22. 21 ad Eustoch.); St. Peter Chrysologus of Ravenna (d. 450) echoes the same teaching: "Woman now is truly made through grace Mother of the living, who had been by nature the mother of the dying." The same teaching can be found in St. Cyril of Jerusalem (d. 386) and St. Ephrem the Syrian (d. 378).

Clearly, this doctrine of Mary as Mother of God and Second Eve is the heart of patristic Mariology. But notice what all this implies. Eve began her life and vocation as "mother of all the living" in a state of innocence, in a state of grace, without any wound or corruption of original sin. Can we imagine that the Blessed Virgin Mary, whose vocation was to be Mother of the Redeemer and of all the redeemed, received a *lesser* grace in preparation for her singular vocation?

It was John Henry Cardinal Newman who best expressed this argument for the Immaculate Conception. In *A Letter to the Rev. E. B. Pusey, D.D., on his recent Eirenicon* (1866), Newman wrote:

I ask, was not Mary as fully endowed [with grace] as Eve? Is it any violent inference that she, who was to cooperate in the redemption of the world, at least was not less endowed with power from on high than she who, given as a helpmate to her husband, did in the event but cooperate with him for its ruin? If Eve was raised above human

---

[18] Ibid.

nature by that indwelling moral gift which we call grace, is it rash to say that Mary had a greater grace? And this consideration gives significance to the Angel's salutation to her as "full of grace" – an interpretation of the original word which is undoubtedly the right one as soon as we resist the common Protestant assumption that grace is a mere external approbation or acceptance, answering to the word "favour," whereas it is, as the Fathers teach, a real inward condition of super-added quality of soul. And if Eve had this supernatural inward gift given her from the first moment of her personal existence, is it possible to deny too that Mary had this gift from the very first moment of her personal existence? I do not know how to resist this inference: – well, this is simply and literally the doctrine of the Immaculate Conception. I say the doctrine of the Immaculate Conception is in substance this, and nothing more or less than this . . . and it really does seem to me to be bound up in that doctrine of the Fathers, that Mary is the Second Eve.[19]

Newman's argument here taken all by itself, is not logically "air-tight". It is an argument of the form "it seems fitting that" or "it is likely that" Mary would be given at least the same endowment of grace from the start of her life as Eve was given. Nevertheless, the argument is strengthened when taken together with other intimations from the ancient Tradition of Mary's all-holy origin.

First of all, there are certain statements of the ancient Eastern Fathers that are simply incomprehensible unless they imply that Mary was full of the grace of the Holy Spirit right from the start of her personal existence. How else can one interpret the words of the fifth century Patriarch of Constantinople St. Proclus, who wrote that Mary was "formed from stainless clay" (Orat. VI: PG 65, 733; cf. 751-756) or the clear witness of St. Ephrem the Syrian (d. 373), who wrote "those two innocent . . . women, Mary and Eve, had been [created] utterly equal, but afterwards one became the cause of our death, the other the cause of our life."[20] St. Ephrem

---

[19] Ibid., 11.
[20] Miravalle, *Introduction to Mary*, 40.

also wrote in his Nisbene Hymns (no. 27): "Truly you, Lord, and your mother are the only ones who are beautiful, completely so in every respect; for there is no spot in you, nor any spot at all in your mother."[21] How could Mary's soul be said to be "*completely*" beautiful in "*every*" respect if her soul bore the wound and corruption of original sin: that is, if her soul was afflicted by a clouded mind, weakened will, and disordered passions – in other words, the broken human condition passed down to us from Adam?

> Some of the later Eastern Fathers are equally explicit. St. Andrew of Crete (d. 720), for example, wrote in his "Canon on the Nativity of the Blessed Mother" (odes 4 and 5): "Today, O Savior, you have given to pious Anne fruitful offspring of her womb, Your Immaculate Mother . . . O Virgin undefiled, undefiled is your birth." Thus, according to St. Andrew, St. Anne's offspring (Mary) was already "immaculate" and "undefiled" at her birth.[22]

St. John Damascene (d. 749) wrote in one of his homilies that "the Holy Spirit came upon Our Lady and hallowed and sanctified her" at the Annunciation (PG 94, 835; cf. PG 96, 704). Does St. John Damascene mean that she was healed of the wound of original sin at the Annunciation rather than at her conception? The Greek verb that he used here, "kathagnizo," can mean to "cleanse," "sanctify," "hallow," or "dedicate." In fact, St. John Damascene uses the same verb in a hymn in honor of our Lady (PG 96, 852), and there it evidently means to "hallow" or "dedicate" rather than to cleanse from sin. Catholics would not necessarily deny that Mary received an *increase* of sanctifying grace at the Annunciation, as a result of the "overshadowing" of the Holy Spirit and the Incarnation of the divine Son in her womb (Lk 1:35). It is clear that this is probably all that St. John Damascene had in mind as well, because in the very same homily (96, 676), he states: "God made Mary the image of all holiness in which he could take delight, because this soul was *always* directed only to God, and *always* turned away from sin's par-

---

[21] As quoted in John R. Willis, S.J., ed., *The Teachings of The Church Fathers* (San Francisco: Ignatius Press, 2002).

[22] Jurgens, *The Faith of the Early Fathers*, vol. III, 326.

ent [the devil]." The word "always" here is most significant, for it implies that by God's grace, from the first moment of her existence until the very end of her earthly life, Mary was preserved from all sin, and even all inclination to sin, her whole being "directed only to God" and "away from" the devil. That is precisely what the Catholic Church means by Our Lady's "Immaculate Conception." Clearly, St. John Damascene's language here is incompatible with any idea that Mary inherited the corruption of original sin, an inherited wound which directs and inclines one *away* from God and *toward* the Devil![23]

In short, what we find in the writings of the Eastern Fathers is an intuitive penetration of the deepest mystery of the Blessed Virgin Mary, the Second Eve. The ancient Fathers have not yet "spelled out" this mystery discursively; rather, they grope for words to be able to articulate what they sense with the intuition of faith, and there can be no mistaking the implications of these words: Mary is, quite simply, "holy origin, point of departure of the new creation" in Christ. As such, her origin could be nothing other than a work of pure, divine grace.

We find an echo of this intuition in the Eastern liturgical traditions as well. The feast of the Conception of the Blessed Virgin Mary, for example, was already being celebrated in the Greek Church in the seventh century. The normal practice, both East and West, was to celebrate the death of an apostle or a saint, their "heavenly birthday," so to speak. Nevertheless, the Eastern churches celebrated the nativity of St. John the Baptist, who was sanctified in his mother's womb (Lk. 1:41). In addition, they celebrated the "conception" of Mary in the womb of her mother, St. Anne. It was from the East that this celebration passed into the Latin Church during the Middle Ages.

Moreover, from the earliest centuries, the Eastern liturgies repeatedly hailed the Blessed Virgin as "Panagia" (all-

---

[23] Englert, *Catholics and Orthodox,* 74-75.

holy one), "Achranatos" (the one without even the slightest stain) and "hypereulogoumene" (the one blessed beyond all others). How can Mary be called *all*-holy, without *any* stain, if from the first moment of her existence she carried within her that inner disorder and corruption, that inclination to sin that both East and West agree is passed down to us from Adam and Eve? Once again, within the ancient Tradition we find intimations – seeds if you will – of the doctrine of the Immaculate Conception.

V.   Common Objections to the Doctrine

There is no reason to review here the long centuries of Catholic discussion and debate about the Immaculate Conception, a debate which generally pitted the Dominicans against the Franciscan and Jesuit proponents of the doctrine for over half a millennium. Ironically, the more the doctrine gained ground in the Catholic Church, the more it lost ground in the East. The first prominent voice in the Greek Church against the doctrine was Nikephoros Xanthopoulous in the fifteenth century, who in his "Commentary on the Feast Days" taught that Our Lady was made immaculate on the day of the Annunciation. In the seventeenth century, John Nathaniel, in his "Skrizhal" (Book of Laws) propagated Xanthopoulous' views. Fr. Clement Englert comments on this situation as follows:

> When Nathaniel's *Skrizhal* appeared in Russia there was a loud outcry against his views on the Immaculate Conception. Especially incensed were the Staroviery or "old-believers" who were devoted to the maintenance of all ancient customs and beliefs, no matter how small or seemingly inconsequential. Accordingly, their opposition to Nathaniel is of special value because of their anger at his violation of ancient [Russian] tradition.[24]

Today, most Orthodox theologians and apologists reject the doctrine of the Immaculate Conception, for various reasons and with varying degrees of insistence. A survey of their objections makes a fitting summary of the case against the

---

[24] Ibid., 73.

doctrine, along with the objections made by Protestant Evangelical writers.

1). Some Evangelicals object to the Immaculate Conception on the grounds that Scripture teaches, in several places, the universal "falleness" of humanity: "There is no one righteous, no not one" (Ps. 14:1-3; 53); "All have sinned and fallen short of the glory of God" (Rom. 3:23); and "through one man's offence, judgment came to all men" (Rom. 5:18). But the Bible often uses broad language, even hyperbole, in order to make a point. For example, when the Bible says "all have sinned" or "all we like sheep have gone astray," it obviously does not intend to include children, who have never committed any personal sins (and if they die before attaining the age of reason, never will). Again, when the Bible says "as in Adam all die, even so in Christ shall *all* be made alive" (1 Cor. 15:22) it evidently does not mean to tell us that the whole human race will be saved in Christ. The passages in Scripture which speak of the universal "falleness" of the human race, therefore, may be said to refer to the mass of mankind in general, without excluding special cases such as the Blessed Virgin Mary (preserved from the wound of original sin) and little children (not yet guilty of actual sin).

2). Fr. Michael Pomazansky, in his classic work *Orthodox Dogmatic Theology*, wrote: "One must acknowledge that the very principle of a preliminary 'privilege' [for Mary] is somehow not in harmony with Christian concepts, for 'there is no respect of persons with God' (Rom. 2:11)."[25] In this passage from Romans, however, St. Paul merely tells us that special privileges and graces, such as those given to the Jews, do not guarantee salvation. Jew and Gentile alike must cooperate with grace and *obey* God if they are to find salvation – which, in fact, they all failed to do! Mary, too, had to freely surrender to, and cooperate with the grace she was given if she was to attain salvation. In her case, however, the grace she was given preserved her from the wound and corruption

---

[25] Father Michael Pomazansky, *Orthodox Dogmatic Theology* (Platina, California: St. Herman of Alaska Brotherhood, 1994), 194.

of original sin in order to prepare her for her special vocation as the Second Eve and the Mother of God. Again, special graces *are* sometimes given by God to those to whom He entrusts special responsibilities.

3). Fr. Pomazansky wrote: "God did not deprive mankind, even after its fall, of His grace-giving gifts, as for example, the words of the 50th Psalm indicate: 'Take not Thy Holy Spirit from me . . .,' or Psalm 70."[26] Fr. Pomazansky here points to a difference between East and West in their understanding of the doctrine of "original sin." All generally agree that the result of Adam's sin was that he bequeathed to his posterity a wounded, disordered human nature, including a clouded mind, weakened will, disordered passions (concupiscence), and a liability to suffering and death. Where the two traditions diverge is that the Latin Church saw all these wounds as symptoms, so to speak, of Adam's loss of the Holy Spirit and sanctifying grace. The East drew no such conclusion.

Of course, everyone recognizes that the Spirit of God was at work in the Old Testament patriarchs and prophets before the coming of Jesus Christ. But Catholics would argue that in whatever way the Holy Spirit was at work in the world prior to the coming of Christ, nevertheless, the Church needs a special outpouring of the Holy Spirit at Pentecost, and each soul does need a special outpouring of that same pentecostal Spirit in Baptism and Confirmation (chrismation). Surely, in some sense there was a general privation of the abiding gift and graces of the Holy Spirit apart from/prior to the coming of Christ, and Catholics believe that Mary, from the very moment of her conception, was completely preserved from it.

4). Orthodox Bishop Kallistos Ware, in his book *The Orthodox Way*, pointed to another (alleged) difference between Catholic and Eastern Orthodox understandings here:

> Orthodoxy does not envisage the fall in Augustinian terms, as a taint of original guilt. If we Orthodox had accepted the Latin view

---

[26] Ibid., 193.

of original guilt, then we might also have felt the need to affirm a doctrine of The Immaculate Conception … the Latin dogma seems to us not so much erroneous as superfluous.[27]

The strength of Bishop Ware's objection depends upon what he understands by Catholic teaching concerning the "guilt" of original sin which we all receive from Adam. The Catholic Church certainly does not mean "guilt" here that everyone who inherits Adam's fallen condition also shares in his personal moral responsibility for original sin (see *Catechism* 403-405). What we share in is the full *effect* of his sin: this includes the loss of the gift of the Holy Spirit and sanctifying grace from our hearts. God made humanity as one corporate entity, one interdependent race with one parental source – Adam and Eve. When our first parents fell from grace, they separated their posterity from grace as well. Thus, the doctrine of the Immaculate Conception was not invented to preserve Mary from any share in personal responsibility for Adam's sin.

We might well ask: where is the proof that every descendent of Adam is born into the world deprived of the gift of the Holy Spirit and sanctifying grace? To be sure, there are hints of this in Scripture (e.g., the much disputed passage, Romans 5:12-19). Above all, the ancient practice of infant Baptism makes little sense if it is not done to restore the life of the Holy Spirit in the soul. After all, infant Baptism does not immediately heal a child of any of the other inherited effects of Adam's sin – not ignorance, concupiscence, suffering, or death. What sacramental gift could be bestowed in infant baptism if not the restoration of the life of the Spirit? The more the baptized soul then freely surrenders to that Spirit – to His gifts, graces, and guidance – the more the other effects of original sin can be tempered and overcome.

The singular gift given to Mary – her Immaculate Conception – was therefore, in certain respects, the equivalent of her infant Baptism, except that she received an out-

---

[27] Bishop Kallistos Ware, *The Orthodox Way* (London: Mowbray, 1979), 102.

pouring of the Holy Spirit at the moment of her *conception* rather than after her birth, and so the effects of original sin were never able to take root in her. Nevertheless, Mary is truly the first among the baptized, the first to be washed in the blood of the Lamb and receive the outpouring of the Spirit (Rom. 5:5, 1 Cor. 12:13).

5). Bishop Ware, in his famous book *The Orthodox Church*, writes: "[The Orthodox] suspect the doctrine [of the Immaculate Conception] because it seems to separate Mary from the rest of the descendents of Adam, putting her in a completely different class from all the other righteous men and women of the Old Testament."[28]

A Catholic reply here would be that the gracious preservation of Mary from the inherited wound of Original sin no more separates her from the people of Israel than the outpouring of the Holy Spirit that St. John the Baptist received in the womb of his mother cuts *him* off from the vocation of Israel. Original sin was never an essential part of the Old Covenant! Rather, it was the main factor that *prevented* the proper fulfillment of that covenant by the people of Israel. In fact, any Jew who receives, welcomes, and follows the Messiah, as Mary did, actually completes and perfects in his own person the true vocation of Israel, which was their calling to become the faithful people of the Messiah (Lk. 1:54-55, 67-75).

6). Archbishop Maximovitch points out that many of the Fathers directly indicate that the Virgin Mary, just as all men, endured a battle with sinfulness, but was victorious over temptations and was saved by her divine Son."[29] However, to say that Mary struggled against temptation is not to imply that she struggled because of any innate sinful inclination within her stemming from the inherited corruption of original sin. After all, our Lord Himself was free from the wound of original sin, yet He was frequently tempted by the Devil (Mt. 4:1; Heb. 2:18, 3:15). Even so, throughout her life, Mary

---

[28] Timothy Ware, The Orthodox Church (Middlesix: Penguin, 1980), 264.
[29] Maximovitch, *The Orthodox Veneration of the Mother of God*, 38-39.

must have had to overcome the snares of the devil, yet this does not necessarily imply that she inherited the corruption of original sin.

7). Archbishop Maximovitch wrote: "This teaching denies all her virtues. After all, if Mary by that grace was preserved from sin even after her birth, then in what does her merit consist?"[30]

Just to clarify: Mary was preserved from the stain of original sin (that is: from that privation of the Holy Spirit and sanctifying grace that results in a disordered human nature and an inclination to sin); she was not preserved from freedom of the will, nor from her responsibility to cooperate with grace and surrender her will in faith and love to the Lord. It was precisely the grace of the Holy Spirit in her soul that enabled her freely to make such a surrender (e.g., at the Annunciation), and it is in this surrender that her merit consists.

8). Archbishop Maximovitch tries to turn the Latin tradition against itself on this matter by arguing that both St. Augustine and St. Ambrose include Mary among those infected with the taint of original sin:

> Blessed Augustine writes: "As for other men, excluding him who is the cornerstone, I do not see for them any other means to become temples of God and to be dwellings of God apart from spiritual rebirth, which must be absolutely preceded by fleshly birth" (Letter 187) . . . [St. Ambrose] teaches . . . the universality of original sin, from which Christ alone is an exception" (commentary on Luke, c. 2, and *Concerning Marriage and Concupiscence,* book 2: against Julianus).[31]

However, Archbishop Maximovitch is simply mistaken about St. Augustine, for St. Augustine clearly states in *Nature and Grace,* 36.42 (CSEL 60):

> Having excepted the Holy Virgin Mary, concerning whom, on account of the honour of the Lord, I wish to have absolutely no question when treating of sins – for how do we know what abundance of

---

[30] Ibid., 45.
[31] Ibid., 41-42.

grace for the total overcoming of sin was conferred upon her, who merited to conceive and bear Him in whom there was no sin?

St. Augustine does not teach here the doctrine of the Immaculate Conception, but that doctrine may be said to fit with his speculation concerning the singular "abundance" of grace given to Mary for the "total" overcoming of sin.

St. Ambrose also does not clearly teach the doctrine of the Immaculate Conception, but neither does he clearly contradict it. In his *Commentary on Psalm 18* (22.30), for example, St. Ambrose calls Mary "a Virgin not only undefiled, but a Virgin whom grace has made inviolate, free of every stain of sin."

9). Finally, Archbishop Maximovitch observes that "There was a difference of opinion [about the Immaculate Conception] even among the most renowned theologians of the West, the pillars, so to speak of the Latin Church. Thomas Aquinas and Bernard of Clairvaux decisively censured it."[32]

Actually, St. Thomas and St. Bernard objected to Medieval forms of the doctrine which were substantially different from the final form defined by Bl. Pope Pius IX in 1854. Many of the Medieval Latin theologians objected to the Immaculate Conception on the grounds that it implied that Mary was not in need of redemption. It was not until Bl. John Duns Soctus (d. 1308) put forward the theory of "Preservative Redemption" that the doctrine could be clearly understood and debated. It follows that we have no right to say that St. Thomas and St. Bernard ever objected to the doctrine subsequently defined by the Church, for with this form of the doctrine St. Thomas and St. Bernard had not the slightest acquaintance!

VI.   The Immaculate Conception and the Analogy of Faith

Let us summarize our argument so far: the dogma of the Immaculate Conception of the Blessed Virgin Mary is best

---

[32] Ibid., 36.

understood and defended as a proper "development of doctrine," from its initial "seeds" in the apostolic Scriptures and ancient, patristic Tradition, until what was implicit in those seeds came to full flower, full explication, by later saints and theologians, and by the Church's Magisterium in the papal definition of 1854. To be sure, the theological arguments that I have presented here are not logically coercive; the arguments have the character not of a series of air-tight deductions, like the links of a chain, but of a series of converging evidences, like the legs upholding the seat of a chair. Just as no single leg of a chair can hold up the chair on its own, so no single piece of evidence, on its own, provides a non-Catholic Christian with an irrefutable argument for the doctrine of the Immaculate Conception. Nevertheless, there is a strong *cumulative* case for the doctrine, based on the *converging evidences and indications* that we have explored from Scripture and ancient Tradition. Quite apart from the whole matter of papal teaching authority, therefore, an Orthodox or Protestant Evangelical Christian might come on these grounds to believe in the Immaculate Conception as a matter of "moral certainty," in other words, as we say in the law courts, "true beyond a reasonable doubt."

However, if we were to end our discussion here, we would have left out two of the most important aspects of the doctrine, aspects that commend the doctrine to the Catholic faithful, and at the same time make it a potentially unifying center of ecumenical dialogue. For as I intimated before, the doctrine of Mary's Immaculate Conception, rightly understood, says something about the nature of the Church dear to the heart of the Orthodox East, and something about God's saving grace dear to the heart of the Evangelical West.

1). Following in the footsteps of St. Paul, Protestant Evangelicals traditionally have sought to show how every mystery of the Faith expresses the saving mercy of God. "To know Christ is to know His benefits," the Lutheran

Melancthon had claimed. Speculative theology is of little value if its conclusions fail to glorify God's free grace and mercy. And yet, properly understood, that is precisely what Mary's Immaculate Conception magnifies most of all! Permit me to quote at length something I wrote for the Congregation of Marians' website a couple of years ago:

> After all, what is Divine Mercy? It is God's undeserved, unmerited, often even unsought for divine grace – the grace that our compassionate God pours out upon us to help us overcome our miseries, and meet our true needs. Theologians call one form of that mercy God's "prevenient" grace, from the Latin "prae-venire" which means "to come before." In other words, even before we ask for it, and quite apart from the fact that we do not deserve it, and have not earned it in the least, God graciously takes the initiative and comes to our aid. Prevenient grace is this completely free gift of God's mercy. We see a faint reflection of it in a parent's love for a child. A child is loved by its parents not because the child had "earned" it, or deserved it, or even asked for it in any way. Rather, the parent's love comes right from the start, a completely free gift, just because the child is the parents' own child. That is human mercy "par excellence," and it is a mirror image of the divine.

When you think about it, that is exactly what is on display in the Immaculate Conception of the Blessed Virgin Mary. The Immaculate Conception is really the supreme manifestation of God's prevenient, unmerited Mercy. After all, Mary did not "merit" her Immaculate Conception. Nor could she ask for it. It was something done in her and for her by the Father of Mercy, and solely on the basis of the foreseen merits of His incarnate Son, Jesus Christ. As Pope John Paul II wrote in his encyclical *Dives in Misericordia* (*Rich in Mercy*), section 9: "Mary is the one who experienced mercy in an exceptional way – as no one else." Fr. Seraphim Michalenko, M.I.C., relying on the work of the French theologian, M.D. Phillippe, once explained the matter this way:

> The mystery of the Immaculate Conception . . . is the expression of the first act of the heavenly Father's mercy in Mary's regard –

an act of absolute gratuity. This is why we can see in it the Father's mercy in its pure state. The first act is the Father's prevenient mercy for this very tiny child that is to be born.

In fact, we can go further and say that the Immaculate Conception of the Blessed Virgin Mary was the great divine act of grace that lay at the foundation of God's whole work of salvation through Christ. The Father of Mercy took the initiative with sinful mankind, fashioning Mary's soul from the moment of conception, preserving it from the effects of original sin, making her soul the very masterpiece of His Mercy, and it was this unique and extraordinary foundation of grace in Mary's soul that enabled her, years later, to respond to the angel Gabriel's message with total, trustful surrender: "Behold the handmaid of the Lord, be it unto me according to Thy word." By God's prevenient grace, therefore, she was made the masterpiece of the Father's Mercy, and in the fullness of time, this special grace within her enabled her to receive our Savior into the world. In short, the whole world's salvation began with a foundational act of unmerited, unprompted, freely given Divine Mercy: that act of mercy was Mary's Immaculate Conception.

2). For the Orthodox tradition of the Christian East, the Church is the manifestation of the eternal in time, of heaven in the midst of our poor earth. This is especially true of the Holy Eucharist, in which our heavenly Lord and all the saints are truly in our midst, manifest in the Real Presence of the risen Christ in the consecrated bread and wine, and in the holy icons of the saints (veritable "windows into heaven"). Here, in the Eucharist, the Bride is one with her heavenly Bridegroom. Here the Church is most fully herself. Here, at least, the Lord receives a true response of love to His eternal love.

Or does He? The Church's life of worship, at least in its temporal aspect, is surely not yet fully sanctified. All too often there are hypocrites at her holy altars, distracted and indifferent worshippers in the pews – some even eat and drink the Body and Blood of the Lord unworthily, in a state of unrepentant mortal sin, to their own condemnation (1 Cor. 11:26-32). Even where there is not outward misconduct, there is the internal disorder caused by original sin. In the very Eucharist itself, therefore, the members of the Church carry the wounds of original and actual sin. If the Church in its life of worship was meant to be the "earthly heaven" (as Kallistos Ware put it), then where on earth can such a truly heavenly offering of worship be found? Perhaps the answer is: "nowhere." Perhaps a true and full response to the love of Christ is impossible on this poor earth, and possible only in heaven.

The very iconography of the Orthodox sanctuary, however, proclaims that this is not so! The Church even on earth has been, one time, fully herself, fully responsive and surrendered to the gracious love of her heavenly Bridegroom.[33] This mystery is proclaimed in the icons of the Annunciation on the royal doors of many an iconostasis; it is proclaimed in the icon of the Orans in many a Byzantine apse. It was proclaimed also in the prophetic words of the Song of Songs (4:7-8, 6:8):

> You are wholly beautiful, my beloved, and without a blemish . . .
> One is my dove, my perfect one is but one, she is the only one of her mother, the chosen of her that bore her. The daughters saw her and declared her most blessed . . .

The words of this great canticle have always been read as descriptive of the love relationship between the Church, or the individual Christian soul, and her heavenly Bridegroom. Yet neither the Church nor any Christian soul on earth has ever been "perfect," "wholly beautiful," or without any "blemish" of original or actual sin. As Fr. Rene Laurentin wrote:

> The promise of God is not empty. Where could it be realized if not in the one who had been chosen as the point of departure for Christ, the Church, and the new creation? The Church itself is made up of sinners. It is in Mary alone that she is holy and without stain.[34]

---

[33] See Pope Paul VI, Apostolic Exhortation *Marialis Cultus*, Section II, no. 16-23: "The Blessed Virgin as the Model of the Church in Divine Worship."

[34] Rene Laurentin, *A Year of Grace with Mary* (Dublin: Veritas, 1987), 95.

HOW DOES THE IMMACULATE CONCEPTION RELATE TO EVERY HUMAN CONCEPTION?

Sr. M. Timothy Prokes, F.S.E., Ph.D.

Introduction

In the parable of the crafty steward (Lk. 16:8) Jesus observes that " . . .the sons of this world are wiser in their generation than the sons of light."[1] Recently, I was reminded how aptly that observation applies to the name chosen by the Church to designate the Marian mystery we are celebrating: The Immaculate Conception. There are believing Catholics who are sometimes uncomfortable with the phrase that names that Marian mystery. Yet, even unconsciously perhaps, there is a strange "coincidence of opposites" that can occur in the naming of a secular event and a mystery of faith. I would like to begin with a modern-day parable, concerning a football game in relation to the Immaculate Conception.

On December 23, 1972, the Pittsburgh Steelers were competing with the Oakland Raiders in an American Football Conference Divisional playoff game at Three Rivers Stadium in Pittsburgh. The Steelers were losing 7-6 and faced a fourth down, ten-yards-to-go play with 22 seconds left in the game. For anyone acquainted with football, that is a do-or-die situation. Their quarterback, Terry Bradshaw, later said "at first all that could go wrong with the play went wrong," but in a desperation attempt, he fired the ball to a receiver who was simultaneously hit from both sides. In the collision, the football flew backwards about 15 yards, and as the sports writer Harvey Frommer reported: "Seemingly out

---

[1] *The RSV Interlinear Greek-English New Testament.* Alfred Marshall trans. (London, 1972), 309.

of nowhere, Franco Harris caught the ball just off his shoe-tops and raced down the field on his way to the end zone. It was an incredible 42-yard run that completed a 60-yard scoring play."[2] Bewildered officials didn't know how to call it at first, uncertain who had touched it, but after conferring, declared it the winning touchdown.

Twenty-eight years later, a writer for *The Sporting News* reflected on the naming of that play as **"The Immaculate Reception"**:

> Long before "The Catch" or "The Drive " or "The Music City Miracle" or whatever catchphrases folks so readily want to bestow anymore, there was this wondrous event.

> A Pittsburgher named Michael Ord was in a tavern and anointed the play moments later with a nickname taken from a Christmastime Catholic holiday, and his friend Sharon Lovosky telephoned Cope at the television station where the Steelers' announcer also worked, performing commentaries.

> Thus begat the Immaculate Reception.

> Chuck Finder, a Pittsburgh sports writer for the past 15 years, was raised 25 miles southwest of the city – but still in the blacked-out television area back in 1972. A Steelers fan as a youngster, he felt the desperation of that fourth-and-10 situation with 22 seconds remaining. So much so, he picked up a telephone while listening to the radio broadcast and rang up "Dial-a-Prayer." It wasn't something little Jewish boys were supposed to do, but, after the play, he figured High Callings didn't care about denominations or affiliations . . .Just true belief."[3]

Sports, for many people today, focus the dedication, intensity, and rituals that have been diluted or lost for many. The Internet article just quoted also cites the desire of Frenchy

---

[2] Harvey Frommer, "The Immaculate Reception," accessed at http://www.travel-watch.com/tarecp.htm.

[3] "The house that the 'immaculate reception' built," from *The Sporting News: Three Rivers Stadium.* Accessed at http://www.sppportingnews.com/archives/threerivers/reception.html.

Fuqua, a fullback in that game, to have a permanent memorial of that touchdown pass at the former site of Three Rivers Stadium, which is now a parking lot. The article states that Mr. Fuqua wants "something big and bold and shrine-like . . . He wants a sanctuary to the Immaculate Reception. 'That's holy ground,' . . . Even if they end up building a hockey rink there, they should put up some kind of a monument to the area where the Immaculate Reception took place."[4]

This modern parable offers insight into the difficulty that even persons of faith express in receiving and understanding the significance of the Immaculate Conception in relation to every human conception. I would cite the following characteristics and longings that surge from within the human heart at times of crisis :

1) There is a seemingly irreversible situation of loss;

2) There is an intervention, inexplicable in the normal range of human events;

3) It is an intervention beyond human conniving and timing;

4) It is a victorious occurrence that involves total bodily receptivity in response to unexpected gift; and

5) It is named and celebrated as a unique event, even among other extraordinary events. In such an earthy example as the football pass we are invited to recognize, parabolically, the immediate significance of this Mystery of faith for all of the conceptions of daily life in the Third Millennium and the inestimable gifts of Divine Mercy waiting for those who receive them and know that "nothing is impossible to God."

When Pope John Paul II officially opened the 150th anniversary year of this dogma on December 8, 2003, he chose to do so at the obelisk erected at the foot of the Spanish Steps in Rome in the nineteenth century when the dogma was first

---

[4] Ibid.

promulgated. I had the privilege of standing there at early dusk this past November. Atop the obelisk, the figure of Mary as the Immaculate Conception rises above the city. Around the base of the obelisk, carved larger than life, are four major Old Testament figures whose missions pointed toward this mystery: Moses, David, Isaiah, and Ezechiel. One of our young Sisters, Sister Raffaella Petrini, whose native home is Rome, brought several of us to the base of the obelisk that November evening, and reflected how fitting it is that this obelisk honoring Mary's Immaculate Conception should rise above this intersection, a place that has been marked by conflict, commercial ventures, and ecclesiastical history. From the obelisk's base flows a melange of life. To one side, a Nike advertisement covers the entire side of a building that houses the Propagation of the Faith (the image of a soccer player leaping across his field of endeavor). Across the piazza are the Tea Rooms where famous poets have met. Kitty-corner are headquarters of a famous clothing stylist, and dropping away from the piazza's fountain is a street described as "The Rodeo Drive" of Rome, where exclusive shops flourish.

Above this confluence of high fashion, commerce, literature, art, and competitive sport rises the image of Our Lady, honored precisely as the "Immaculate Conception." The convergence of so many endeavors of human life comes to an unlikely focal point: the image of one who is totally human, yet totally without sin. The paradox of juxtaposing an inexplicable football play, known in sports history as the "Immaculate Reception," with the nineteenth century sculpture of the Immaculate Conception is helpful in illuminating the ways in which this Marian dogma touches us.

I.   Human Conception

The mystery of Mary's Immaculate Conception relates to every human conception: 1) to the conceiving of human thoughts and plans, or what is more deeply termed "the heart"; and 2) to the conceiving of new, personal, embodied life. *To conceive is to author new life.* The mystery of the Immaculate Conception confirms the ***sinlessness*** of Mary's life from its inception. As we know, Mary is described as conceiving Christ in her heart – that is, at the core of her interior being – before conceiving Him bodily. She personifies, then, as the Church frequently affirms, a sinlessness in both kinds of human conceiving,

What does **sinlessness** mean? Our human life begins (despite the wonder of its fragility and undeveloped capacities to think and choose) in a **still-unchosen** situation of sinfulness. The more we come to know of the human genome and the intricacies of genetic patternings that have been transmitted through generations, the more we realize how deeply our existence is immersed in the lives of all who constitute our genealogy. This should also help us to understand the meaning of original sin and its transmission through human generations. There is a struggle that penetrates the lived body-person: created to be in total union with God, but bearing from conception the woundedness of separation from God. The gratuitous gift of Baptism heals that basic alienation, but the consequences of having been severely wounded remain. No Pelagian explanation of a peerless coming into existence will endure the light of truth.

A Canadian friend tells with a kind of amazement how the *tendency* to sin is apparent even in small, lovable and loved children. One of his grandchildren, a child of two, had come with her parents for Thanksgiving Dinner. She was noisy, creating a scene at table, to the point where the grandfather was embarrassed for his daughter, the child's mother, who seemingly was oblivious of the child's disruptive antics. Our friend, the child's grandfather, observed quite loudly to his wife: "I wonder if Annie is tired or sick." Relating this later, he rather marveled at the two-year-old's response. She had heard his comment, drawn herself up, and announced "I'm not tired. I'm not sick. I'm being bad for nothing!"

Since we are all conceived in original sin, it is difficult to comprehend adequately what it means to be "immaculately conceived." Perhaps that is partially why some find it difficult to affirm the mystery. **The Immaculate Conception means Mary's loving union with God from the beginning of her existence** – the freedom from anything that would separate her from God – and a freedom from anything that would be a barrier to the love of every other human person. It means, in practical terms, that there is no deception, no self-serving plans or motives, no attempt to take advantage of others or harm them in any way. It is to be love enfleshed in an appropriate expression of self-gift, to be the peerless human image of God.

In a sense, we begin life at the opposite end of the spectrum from Mary. She was conceived without sin and lived out a totally sinless self-gift despite the challenges, difficulties, and anguish that her life entailed. All other human persons begin life affected by sin, and are called to move, in "grace upon grace," to ever more complete and chosen sinlessness. For Mary, however, it was the completely unexpected, totally gratuitous intervention of God, anticipating her Son's future redemption, that preserved her from any taint of sin from the first moment of her existence. For every other human person, it is Baptism that removes all that separates from God, or would compete with God, but leaving concupiscence, the inclination to sin.

For us, then, there is the call, in grace, to move *toward* ever- intensified sinlessness. In so doing, we enter ***partially*** into the characteristics of Mary's Immaculate Conception. Snatched from seemingly sure defeat by an inexplicable intervention beyond human powers; through Baptism there is a divine gift received which requires free response and resolve. We come into life paradoxically: conceived in a state of original sin, yet destined for sinless union with God. Into this mystery comes the gift of Mary's Immaculate Conception, and all that it illumines concerning own journey in light of her Son's Redemption. Mary's gift has to do with beginnings. From that particular vantage point, what does that mean for every human conception?

II.   Immaculately Conceiving in Thought and Plan

First, then, how can we move ever more deeply into the mystery of conceiving immaculately "in heart" – that is, not only within the interior faculties of intellect, will, imagination, and memory, but even within that deep interiority that exceeds our own striving – to that impenetrable depth called "the heart" or "the inner spirit"? As the Second Vatican Council stressed, there is a universal call to holiness. Realized holiness, indeed, means that nothing willfully-chosen separates a person from God. Such a communion of persons, human with divine, can only be realized through a graced life of ever greater transparency in truth and love. Father Peter John Cameron, O.P., in a magnificent editorial in the *Magnificat* for December, 2003, writes:

> The Immaculate Conception is our "pattern of holiness." As the preface for this solemnity proclaims, Mary is more exemplar than role model. We can never match the unique blessedness that Mary is given as a pure, ineffable gift from God at the moment of her conception. But we can partake in that blessedness when we allow Mary to be "the mold designed to form and shape God-like creatures" (Saint Louis de Montfort). Everything that God brings about in Mary he does for us. It is for love of us that God made Mary so exalted (Julian of Norwich) . . .The mystery of the Immaculate Conception could have remained God's Great Secret. But then the certainty of divine mercy would have remained "inconceivable." God discloses his secret through the Church's defined dogma of the Immaculate Conception in order to give us an infallible way to conceive of divine tenderness and clemency. (pp. 4-5)

Our beginnings can only be authentically understood in truth and love, and then only partially, because we are dealing with mystery – a reality so profound that we never fully penetrate it, but only enter more and more deeply. Despite our sinfulness, there is a profound longing for beginnings that are not immersed in sinfulness. Cardinal Ratzinger dealt with this in his 1991 address *Conscience and Truth*, given to the United States Bishops in Dallas. He described two levels of conscience that must constantly be related to each other: 1) the interior capacity and disposition for observing what has been commanded; and 2) the power of judgment and decision. Appealing to the thoughts of St. John, St. Basil, and St. Augustine, Ratzinger said that the term which proves most apt for designating the first level of conscience is *anamnesis*:

> This means that the first so-called ontological level of the phenomenon conscience consists in the fact that something like an original memory of the good and true (both are identical) has been implanted in us, that there is an inner ontological tendency within man, who is created in the likeness of God, toward the divine. From its origin, man's being resonates with some things and clashes with others. This anamnesis of the origin, which results from the godlike constitution of our being is not a conceptually articulated knowing, a store of retrievable contents. It is so to speak an inner sense, a capacity to recall, so that the one who it addresses, if he is not turned in on himself, hears its echo from within. He sees: That's it! That is what my nature points to and seeks.[5]

While it is interior, said Ratzinger, this anamnesis is instilled in our being – it is an instilled memory that has a *maieutic* function, not imposing what is foreign, but bringing "to fruition what is proper to anamnesis, namely, its interior openness to truth."[6] Recall how Jesus, responding to his questioners regarding divorce pointed to "the beginning" to clarify the divine intent regarding marriage. Pope John Paul II,

[5] Joseph Cardinal Ratzinger, *Conscience and Truth* (Braintree, MA: Pope John Center, 1991), 14
[6] Ibid., 16.

initiating his series of Audiences on marriage, began similarly, by looking to "the beginning."

When we reflect on Mary's Immaculate Conception – the marvel that from the first instance of her life she was in sinless relation with God, full of grace – we can begin to appreciate in some way the significance of that for us, not only as the opening toward her own conception of our Redeemer, Jesus Christ, but as the opening for realizing the importance of every beginning, every conception in our own lives. How complex are beginnings, how fragile! In the conception of our ideas, plans, judgments, and choices, how precious becomes that *anamnesis* – the maieutic, or "midwifing" assistance to remember even in our tendency toward sin – what is at-one, good, true, and beautiful. What holy ground is the living body-person, privileged to conceive daily plans concerning whom to meet, where to go, what to say, write, design, or give away. Each of these conceptions will involve in some way our intentions, our integrity, or lack of it – and every relationship of our lives. Each beginning will have reference in some way to that anamnesis that is either in harmony or disharmony with the original sinless beginning. Or, as Cardinal Ratzinger wrote, the "Christian memory, to be sure, is always learning, but proceeding from its sacramental identity, it also distinguishes from within between what is a genuine unfolding of its recollection and what is its destruction or falsification."[7] How important, then, are the reasons, *the motives, the methods involved in our initiation of what we begin!*

In Mary, the New Eve, there was a renewed beginning for humanity. Each of us can find analogies in our memory of new beginnings, new possibilities, when we receive the gift of morning in each new, unrepeatable day; in taking up the privilege of ever-new tasks, relationships, plans. I sometimes use a homely example with students to underscore the significance of beginnings. In buttoning a cardigan sweater, it is very

---

[7] Ibid.

important that the buttoning follow the "truth of being" of the sweater. If the first button does not meet the truth of the first hole, no matter how rapidly, or how far one keeps buttoning, the whole will be off-kilter. In realizing the error, one must not only skip another button, but return to the original truth of the first, set it right, in order that the rest of the sequence can bear a relationship to the truth of the garment.

When we have chosen what is sinful, it is necessary to return to what needs to be set right, forgiven, healed. The image of Mary as the Immaculate Conception, rising above Rome's Spanish Steps is a marvelous reminder for us, and a point of intercession for all the activity of the world that swirls around the base of the obelisk that marks her mystery. We do not have the gift of her total exception from sin. Nevertheless, it is the pattern we are called to enter by graced choice and a reminder to ask her intercession: Hail Mary, full of grace – *pray for us sinners now and at the hour of our death.*

St. John of the Cross and St. Teresa of Avila have parallel ways of describing the move from sinfulness to sinless union with God. Teresa, in her mature years, described it as a seven-stage journey to the center of one's being, to the Seventh Mansion where the Bridegroom dwells. For the persons he directed, John of the Cross drew the image of Mount Carmel, and the paths leading to its summit where the Bridegroom is. For both, the images indicate a conversion of life, a striving in all of one's human powers, until there is a capacity open to Divine Persons infusing what is beyond human faculties to achieve . . .what for humans is impossible, but for God is possible.

III.   The Significance of this Mystery for Conceiving New Human Life

Perhaps at no other time in Christian history has there been so crucial a need to recognize the way in which the mystery of the Immaculate Conception touches the conceiving of every child. Perhaps, also, at no other time has there been such indifference regarding freedom from sin in the conception of new human life, and such diversity in the *reasoning, motives, and methods* involved. If questions regarding marriage, family, and the conception of children were posed to Jesus in the public square today, would He initiate His reply by once more saying: "It was not so in the beginning . . ."?

When Pope Paul VI issued *Humanae Vitae* in 1968, many "reasoned" that he was wrong in maintaining the unity of life-giving and love-giving in marital acts. To choose to conceive or not conceive a child was perceived by many as a separate issue from marital intercourse as a unitive, love-giving act, the latter defended as more spontaneous, uninhibited, and richer if there could be some assurance that a child would *not* be conceived. This reasoning seemed to be supported by the "right motivation" of responsibly limiting the number of children who could be welcomed and adequately cared for in a changing society. Each "chosen" child would then be given the attention, love, and opportunities that would otherwise be compromised. This reasoning and motivation was accompanied by a plethora of methods that assured feasibility and attainability.

Many in the larger society began to term the availability of such methods "fundamental rights," not to be denied, particularly to women who had been subject to domination, poverty, and legal strictures. Then, it seemed obvious: if methods to prevent conception failed, there should be the additional right to obtain legal abortions. Further, in a permissive society, it seemed evident that young girls who became pregnant should have a right to abortion, with or without parental consent. The rapidity with which all of this occurred would not have been imagined even sixty years ago. I recite this series not to convey any new information, but to bring into reflection what is currently occurring in the conception of children and why it relates to the mystery of Mary's Conception.

We are moving through a time when smallness is prized – not how many angels can dance on the head of a pin, but how many genetic components tiny instruments can manipulate. At the poke of a stylus, palm-pilots handle what once required rooms of computer equipment. There is a great fascination in seeing how much multi-tasking can be accomplished in ever-smaller containers. This ability, and the accompanying fascination it invites, have a paradoxical counterpart in the laboratories where human lives are conceived and where the very minute components of human conception are manipulated with expertise and a fascination with "what can be." Notice how advertisements for fertility centers portray the results of their work in very personalized terms, omitting the technological methods involved.

Sinlessness in the conception of human life is at stake here. To speak in these terms, of course, means a recognition that the conception of a human life is called to be in harmony with a divine meaning and plan. Despite original sin, there remains in that *anamnesis* described by Cardinal Ratzinger, the memory of what from the beginning is good and true, hence beautiful. While the transcendent realities form a unity, the present culture-of-fragmentation tends to separate what seems "good" from what formerly was recognized as "true." In *technological* terms of fashioning human life, to argue for a perceived greater "good" means adjusting what is "true" to fit the situation. The beautiful will then be in the eye of the fabricator.

In reality, the mystery of the Immaculate Conception points to several principles concerning the conception of human life which are particularly pertinent: 1) human life begins at conception; 2) the minute size of a newly-conceived life, fascinating as it is, is not matter for manipulation – it is the mystery of a new human person; and 3) brilliant reasoning, technical competence, and the varying levels of motivation which drive attempts to achieve more perfect "human specimens" do not morally validate the methods employed, even when prospective parents and judges permit, even invite them.

It is astounding in a way that the dogma of the Immaculate Conception was proclaimed at a time when there was so little *scientific* knowledge concerning human conception. How recent is the realization (I will not say "discovery") that each parent contributes equally to the DNA of a newly-conceived child. A living strand from each meets the other in a kind of spiral dance. Sadly, so swiftly following this amazing realization regarding DNA came the notion that the strands of DNA – the elements of life, heritage, and relationship – were now open to addition or omission, depending upon what "results" were sought. This conviction, when applied practically in genetic engineering, proves to be a wedge, opening the mystery of conception to malleable exploitation.

There is a tragic analogy here with Genesis, Chapter III: the integrity of person-gift became distorted at the fountain-head of humanity. It is not surprising, then, that there is distortion in the conception of children apart from the uninhibited body gift of spouses to one another. A man and woman (or any individual who has access to gametes) can hand over responsibility to a technician to effect the conception of a new human life, often in the name of obtaining a desired child. While celebrated as a free choice, it is a devastation of child and parent(s) isolated from the truth of the marital act.

Beyond that, of course, is the refusal of any "beginning" when there is the blocking or killing of gametes which would have the capacity to express mutual bodily self-gift. The elements of self-gift are considered hostile – treated as refuse, toxic materials, or invasive substances. The wonderful capacity to perceive what occurs in the conception of a human life is disfigured.

IV.   Reclaiming the Dignity of Beginnings

Sometimes, even among persons of faith, there is confusion regarding two distinct but related mysteries: 1) Mary's Immaculate Conception, the beginning of her life in her mother Ann's womb, and 2) Mary's conception of Jesus Christ through the overshadowing of the Holy Spirit. While they are distinct realities, there is a marvelous relationship between them, and both have immense bearing on every human conception. The splendor and dignity of every newly-conceived life is manifest in Mary's conceiving of Jesus Christ. The Archangel Gabriel not only conveys to her the revelation that she is called to be the Mother of Jesus. Gabriel also reveals that her cousin Elizabeth has conceived a child at an advanced age "because nothing is impossible to God." (Lk. 1:37) How poignant are Luke's concise statements at the conclusion of Gabriel's message: "And the angel left her," and "Mary set out at that time and went as quickly as she could to a town in the hill country of Judah." (Lk. 1:38 -39)[8]

Luke does not say how many days it took for Mary's journey to Ain Karim, where Elizabeth and Zachary lived in the hill country outside of Jerusalem,. If Mary went "as quickly as she could," the 80-90 mile journey – whether in a caravan or some related manner of travel – would not have taken many days. How diminutive would have been the newly-conceived life that she carried when she received the affirmation of Elizabeth in that mystery we name the Visitation! The dignity of every newly-conceived life is indicated by the greeting that Elizabeth and the unborn John gave to Mary and the so-recently conceived Jesus. Size or stage of womb-development is no determinant of the inestimable value of a child's new life. The six-month old child within Elizabeth's womb leapt at the Presence of the days-old child in Mary's womb. The Visitation was the vibrant meeting of four persons, a meeting which resonates with meaning and the immense dignity of every newly-conceived life. The con-

[8] Translation from *The Jerusalem Bible*, Alexander Jones, gen. ed. (Garden City, NY: Doubleday and Co., 1966).

ception of Jesus is revealed beyond Mary herself through that first meeting of John the Baptist and Jesus while they were still in their mothers' wombs, the Child Jesus so small that His body probably would not yet have been visible to the naked eye.

The only two conceptions which can be termed "immaculate" – that is, free from all sin and in closest union with the Trinity are the conceptions of Mary and of Jesus. If there is a concatenation of **sins** that cascades from the original sin at the beginning of humanity, there is a wonderful flowing of **grace and salvation** through the Immaculate Conception, poured out as gratuitous gift in Mary through the foreseen redemption of her divine Son's enduring Self-gift. Because of her coming-to-be in sinlessness, there was opened the way of our salvation, the future conception of Jesus from whom all graces continue to be given to us.

How holy, then, is the human marital act which is open to the conception of new life! How devastating the vitiation of that act, even when it is done in the name of love, in the name of providing an individual or partners with not only "a" child, but the most perfectly contrived child that technology can assure. The wisdom that moved Pope John Paul II to begin his pontificate by looking to "the beginning," as Christ did, in terms of understanding marriage, continues to bless the Church and all who receive reverently the encyclicals, letters, exhortations that develop and apply the insights conveyed in the early moments of his papacy. John Paul continues to link sinless beginnings with the capacity to discern truth, and its relation to right reason and loving self-gift. The Church speaks of the "coinherence" of the mysteries of faith. Every aspect of truth, every mystery of faith, is intimately united with every other gift in the Deposit of Faith.

In this 150th year of the promulgation of the dogma of the Immaculate Conception it is significant to look at each of our beginnings, each of our conceptions in mind, inner-heart, and body. One of the immense gifts that the Church can bring to the contemporary world is deep joy in beginnings. This does not require exotic events. For the most part, it means openness to the ever-newness of each moment, marked by unique events, days, and seasons. **Every new day is a beginning, absolutely fresh in creation**, open to new response in love and truth, in a resolve toward sinlessness. Every reception of the Sacrament of Reconciliation, particularly, invites wonder at forgiveness and the affirmation "to sin no more." Every morning's awakening is a fresh return to family, community, or job, offering a beginning that will either be immersed in sin, or dedicated in love.

A more intense term than "dedication" is "consecration." To be *consecrated* is to be "set apart" for God. Consecration is the act of designating persons or material beings as given and ordered to God. This may be expressed publicly, as in sacramental life, by blessing, vowing – sometimes anointing – whatever is being consecrated or dedicated to God. There is a basic principle here: *one cannot dedicate or consecrate to God* what is sinful. Whatever is to be offered in praise, thanks, and love to God, cannot stem from sinfulness. It is obvious, for example, that such things as suicide bombings and dishonest financial dealings are not suitable for dedication to God. The principle is less obvious, however, when there are plans to conceive human life to assuage an ardent desire to "have a child" or when arguments are advanced for the conception of embryos for research that may benefit Alzheimer patients.

In a sin-conditioned world, efforts to attain a *perceived good* can lead to cynicism regarding integrity, to a kind of "picking at the hem of mystery" to distortions of truth, goodness, and beauty. For example, close to the Feast of the Immaculate Conception in 2003, a billboard was posted in East Providence, Rhode Island by PETA (People for the Ethical Treatment of Animals) which used an image of the

Blessed Mother holding a dead chicken, with the wording "Go Vegetarian. It's an Immaculate Conception."[9] Sponsors of the message claimed that "Religious-based messages resonate with people," and "We're still at a loss for why it was offensive . . . If people are offended because Mary is holding a carcass of a chicken, maybe it's because they are eating carcasses of chickens." After all, the spokesman said, the image of Mary was respectful and "beautifully drawn." The inability to see the significance of a concept in relation to larger truth, goodness, and beauty is an enduring difficulty in a culture that, on the one hand, intuitively knows the power of genuine symbols, and on the other hand, exploits those symbols to market personal agendas.

Beginnings have an inherent excitement and promise that sometimes make assessments of integrity difficult. It is important to recognize two things. First, it is difficult to feel restraint when there is fresh promise and excitement in new conceptions – whether these are conceptions in our interior powers of intellect, will, imagination, and memory or conceptions of new human life. Second, when there has been a false start, and the later rueful realization that something has been sinfully conceived, it is also difficult to admit this. It can seem easier simply to continue the charade or justify what has begun sinfully. It is essential to know two further realities: 1) one sinful beginning is not healed by further sinful acts; and 2) the mercy of God is far greater than any of our puny sinful disruptions of the universe.

Let us make that concrete. If a child has been conceived apart from the integrity of a marital act – whether body-to-body or under laboratory conditions, it is crucial that the child be received, with the recognition that it has already been wounded by those accountable for its conception, whether this has been through irresponsible seeking of pleasure, the desire to possess a child for one's own benefit, or the planned con-

[9] Catholic News Service, "Billboard Equating Vegetarianism with Immaculate Conception Removed," in *Arlington Catholic Herald* (December 11. 2003), 19.

trivance of technicians. If a child has already suffered aspects of sinfulness in its beginnings, these are not overcome by further sin and rejection. Love and reliance on the guidance and mercy of God are especially due to these children. The mystery of the Immaculate Conception, promised at the dawn of humanity's creation, is echoed in the image of Mary atop the obelisk of the Immaculate Conception. Its foundation is embedded in the swirling, often sinfully conceived events of daily life, but not overcome by them.

V.   Light and Receptivity

Reflection on the immense privilege we have in relating every human conception to this Marian dogma suggests two tangible ways of marking this anniversary symposium: through image and sacrament.

First, what image can be an ongoing reminder of the mystery? Genesis says with liturgical solemnity: "Now the earth was a formless void, there was darkness over the deep, and God's spirit hovered over the water. **God said 'Let there be light and there was light. God saw that light was good, and God divided darkness from light.'**" (Gn. 1:2-3) The Divine Word opens creation with light, even though sun and moon are specifically designated as given on the fourth day. In the Nicene Creed, the Church professes Jesus Christ, the One who became incarnate for us through Mary as "God from God, Light from Light." Why is **light** such a powerful way of naming Jesus Christ? The writers of *Lumen Gentium*, the Second Vatican Council's Dogmatic Constitution on the Church, open the document by proclaiming anew that Christ is the "Light to the Nations." What is there about Light that opens us to the mystery of Jesus Christ, and also to the mystery regarding Mary's sinlessness and the goodness of creation?

We are familiar with the image of light being associated with goodness, truth, and holiness. The brochure for this symposium features the image of Mary emanating rays of light. For two millennia, artists have represented the holiness of Christ, Mary, saints, and angels, through halos or bursts of light. In fact, in recent decades, through the application of certain photographic equipment, it is possible to provide visual evidence that every living person has a kind of "aura."

Several characteristics of light seem to make it an especially fitting image for receiving and entering more deeply into the mystery of the Immaculate Conception. First, light does not exist for its own sake. Second, whatever light shines upon, it discloses the other, not drawing attention to itself, but to the multiple facets of whatever it falls upon. Third, light touches the sordid and disordered as well as the beautiful, illuminating the truth of what it touches without itself becoming sordid or disordered.

Consider, then, how light is a particularly apt sign of the Immaculate Conception. Mary's sinlessness and unbroken fullness of grace, like the light, does not exist for her own sake. Rather, it allows attention to dwell on the truth of whatever it illumines. Created light is a servant creature. It can be focused to a penetrating intensity, to reveal – or to heal, even burn away what is infected or destructive.

Light is impartial in revealing the truth of things – delineating a beloved's face, the intricate design of a meadowlark, the fold upon fold of an opening rose – as well as the ugliness of pornography. Light can penetrate the most sordid of realities, revealing them for what they are without becoming sordid, and without clinging to them. Light can withdraw from what is incredibly evil without itself bearing away a trace of the ugliness. It is one of the purest, most pervasive gifts of creation: transparent, without deception.

It is no wonder, then, that in her apparitions, Our Lady's appearance is often described as luminous, equally at home in a French cove among shepherd children; on a Mexican mountain path; or in the midnight sanctuary of a contemplative convent. Mary could identify herself to the child Bernadette: "I am the Immaculate Conception." As swift and weightless as light, Our Lady does not visit us to convey a new revelation, but to illumine the truths of beings, so that we can distinguish more deeply what *is*. In the middle of night, Mary gave birth to the Light of the world. A star led the Magi to Bethlehem; and the Church affectionately greets Mary as "Star of the Sea." She is the woman with the moon beneath her feet and on her head a crown of twelve stars. It seems apt that the image of light be an ongoing sacramental reminder of her sinlessness. The fresh experience of light each morning is an echo of the first day of the good creation The preciousness of light is enhanced, not quenched by darkness.

VI.   The Sacrament of This Anniversary Year

If **light** is a specific image of Mary's gift, what **sacrament** in particular marks this anniversary year? Surely Baptism is the touchstone of relationship to the Immaculate Conception, but most of us gathered for this Symposium have been baptized. We can more readily identify with the *anamnesis* which Cardinal Ratzinger explains – the memory of original sinlessness that is a constituent part of our consciences. I would suggest that a prime way of marking this anniversary year is a more frequent and more attentive reception of the Sacrament of Reconciliation. Whenever we receive this sacrament, there is a fresh beginning, a renewal of life in closest relation to the mystery of sinlessness. In the past few decades, regular reception of this sacrament has declined in most parishes in the United States. Sadly, the sacrament is not readily accessible in parts of the nation where there is a shortage of priests.

There is need for thoughtful renewal of the realization that only God forgives sin. The wonder is: reception of this sacrament increasingly opens us to the Marian dogma. The

Catechism of the Catholic Church (#1469) cites a portion of Pope John Paul II's *Reconciliatio et paenitentia*:

> It must be recalled that . . . this reconciliation with God leads, as it were, to other reconciliations, which repair the other breaches caused by sin. The forgiven penitent is reconciled with himself in his inmost being, where he regains his innermost truth. He is reconciled with his brethren whom he has in some way offended and wounded. He is reconciled with the Church. He is reconciled with all creation. (*RP* 31,5)

The great consolation is that we can know "immaculate receptions" even when it is the "fourth quarter of life, fourth-and-ten, and 22 seconds to go." A bishop from Saskatchewan related an experience that he had as a newly ordained priest. Assigned to the cathedral parish of the diocese, he responded to night calls for the Last Sacraments from the nearby Catholic Hospital. One night, about 2 a.m., he received an urgent call from the Sister on night duty. She told him that a man from the parish was dying in Room 229. When he heard the patient's name, he winced at the thought of going out in the bitter cold to administer the Last Rites, since this man had caused problems in the parish. He left immediately, however, and went right to the room.

The bishop remembered that he had wasted no time. Coming to the dim-lit bedside, he said to the man: "You know that you are dying. Isn't it about time that you made your peace with God?" Amazingly, the man said yes, and the young priest was able to administer the Sacraments of the Dying. When the priest stepped out into the hallway, a Sister frantically called to him, "Father, come!" He told her not to worry since he had already administered the Sacraments. She said, "No! It's Room 329 upstairs." He followed her and administered the Last Sacraments to the "trouble-maker" from the parish. The first man died, but the second recovered. It was an "Immaculate Reception" kind of experience.

May two concrete realities express our celebration of this anniversary: the image of light and the frequent, more "immaculate reception" of the Sacrament of Reconciliation.

VIRGO ECCLESIA FACTA:

THE IMMACULATE CONCEPTION, ST. FRANCIS OF ASSISI AND THE RENEWAL OF THE CHURCH

Fr. Peter Damian M. Fehlner, F.I., S.T.D.

The title of this essay has been taken from the original Latin text of the *Salute*[1] of St. Francis of Assisi to the Blessed Virgin Mary, a classic of Marian thought and devotion, a direct fruit of the well-known mystical experience of the Poverello of Assisi before the Crucifix of San Damiano in 1206: an experience crucial not only for the life of this saint and the history of the Order of Minors founded by him, but crucial above all for the history of the Church. This Salute is likewise bound up with his love of the little Marian sanctuary known popularly as the "Portiuncula" or little portion of Mary, which became the little portion of Francis because Francis became the portion or possession of Mary Immaculate[2]. Of this further on.

---

[1] All texts of St. Francis are taken from the critical edition of C. ESSER, *Opuscula Sancti Patris Francisci Assiensis* (Bibliotheca Franciscan Ascetica Medii Aevi XII), Grottaferrata 1978. Likewise all references to the Saint's writings are based on this edition. English versions of these writings and of the sources for his life are many and easily available. *1 Cel.* and *2 Cel.* are respectively abbreviations for the *First Life* and *Second Life of St. Francis* by Thomas of Celano. *Leg. Major* designates the complete life of St. Francis by St. Bonaventure.

[2] For a comprehensive, in-depth presentation of the essentially Marian spirituality and apostolate of St. Francis cf. the recent study of J. SCHNEIDER, ofm, *"Virgo Ecclesia facta." Die Gegenwart Marias auf dem Kreuzbild von San Damiano und im* "Officium Passionis" *des Heiligen Franziskus von Assisi* (Rome 1998), soon to appear in English from Academy of the Immaculate, New Bedford MA under the title: *"Virgo Ecclesia facta". The Presence of Mary in the Crucifix of San Damiano and in the* "Office of the Passion" *of St. Francis of Assisi*. Pope John Paul II himself praised this book in 1998 as the best study on Mary published that year. Page references to the English version.

Significant also for this essay underscoring the relevance of the Immaculate Conception for the living faith of the Church is the full title of that small, but ancient sanctuary. It was, and still is, St. Mary of the Assumption, Queen of the Angels. That, too, is the title of the upper Basilica of Assisi designed by the much maligned Br. Elias to give expression to the great portion of Mary and Francis in heaven, as the little portion in the plain beneath Assisi gives expression to their joint portion during a time of pilgrimage. One need only read the sixth chapter of the *Definitive Rule* (Nov. 29, 1223) of St. Francis to recognize that the observation was initially his: desiring naught else, let this be your portion (viz., the poverty of the Mother of Jesus) leading to the land of the living . . . poor in temporal things (the little portion), rich in virtue (anticipation of the glory of the resurrection in heaven, anticipated in Mary by her Assumption and effectively anticipated in the life of grace during a time of pilgrimage through her maternal mediation).

In this way we are brought to see that "living faith" includes not merely an intellectual dimension, important as this is, much less the merely sentimental or emotional experience of confidence, such as fiducial faith in the "faith alone" of Protestantism, but above all entails that distinctive gift of grace which makes of faith the substance of the Church's hope, source of a never failing, ever vibrant, never to be disappointed desire for the coming of the Groom (cf. Rev. 22, 16-21).

Some may wonder why in an essay dealing with the acts of the divinely instituted Magisterium of the Church I should concentrate on the life and work of one saint and on private revelations to him. The answer is very simple: because private revelations and the lived theology of the saints[3], while in no wise "adding" to public revelation are in the providence of God the

---

[3] On the crucial importance of the theology of the saints for all other modes of theologizing cf. F.M. Léthel, ocd, *Connaître l'amour du Christ qui surpasse toute connaissance. La théologie des Saints* (Venasque 1989). For the same in St. Bonaventure, cf. P. Fehlner, "Mater et Magistra Apostolorum", in *Immaculata Mediatrix* 1/1 (2001) 15-54, in particular pp. 31 ff. on the relation of the contemplative mode of theology to the symbolic and speculative modes.

ordinary means for initiating and preparing the way for doctrinal definitions and for renewal of the Church. On both scores this is especially true of St. Francis in relation to the dogma of the Immaculate Conception and the problem of Church "repair", viz., renewal in the face of a mammoth crisis of faith, at root involving the machinations of the "enemy" of the Woman (cf. Gen. 3, 15; Mt. 13, 28. 39; Rev. 12, 1 ff.: where the enemy who sowed the tares in the field which is the world and the Church is the enemy of the Woman, namely the serpent-dragon-prince of this world).

We might devote the rest of this essay just to these points. These few remarks, however, are sufficient to set in relief a key insight to be pondered, like Mary and with Mary in the heart (cf. Lk. 2, 19. 51), whenever the subject of Our Lady and St. Francis and Franciscans is under discussion. The starting point of any such discussion, whether it concern the purpose of the Minorites in the Church or the key features of their life and mission, is never a question of what place is to be assigned Mary in the Franciscan world. Rather, it is always a question of what place St. Francis and Franciscans might have in the world of Mary, of what service they can render to their Queen who has deigned to visit them and make them her *Portiuncula*, in order precisely *to accomplish some service for her as Mother of the Church and Mediatress of all grace*. This service, essentially, is the promotion of the Immaculate Conception: its solemn definition as prelude to its incorporation into the life of the Church via total consecration, as basis for the repair of the Church and for her preparation in view of the second coming and triumph of "the kingdom of the Sacred Heart of Jesus" (St. Maximilian M. Kolbe, *SK* 1331[4])

This can easily be demonstrated with a brief reflection on a popular name for St. Francis, *Poverello*, "little poor man", of Assisi. Poverty (and with it penance), rightly, is commonly recognized as the primary distinguishing feature of Franciscan

---

[4] Citations from St. Maximilian are from the critical Italian edition of his writings: *Scritti di Massimiliano Kolbe* (Rome 1997), abbreviated *SK*, followed by number of work cited.

religious life. Now, if there is one thing which essentially distinguishes the poverty of St. Francis as the poverty of Christ for the sake of the redemption and salvation of souls and of the Church (and not the misery of Marx and liberation theology), it is its Marian quality. By poverty St. Francis understands that of the Virgin Mother, who above all others realizes the first and fundamental beatitude: "blessed are the poor in Spirit, for theirs is the kingdom of heaven."

"In *Spirit*": the beatitudes rightly describe first of all the Virgin Mother of God, overshadowed by the Spirit of Father and Son and so blessed as virginal Mother and maternal virgin, to be called blessed by all generations, including her Son. In his *Definitive Rule*, chapter 6 (and still more clearly in the *Rule* of St. Clare, ch. 6) St. Francis contrasts the conditions of beatitude during the time of pilgrimage and in the state of glory: poor in temporal things yet rich in virtue now, let this be your *portion* which leads into the land of the living (and the riches seen in the Queen crowned with glory). It is this poverty which enables the brothers to love each other with a love more perfect than the love of a mother for her child.

This love is, as St. Clare notes in her Rule, the love of the Mother who out of love for us sacrificed her dearest Son that we might be saved from everlasting death and enjoy eternal beatitude in paradise. Or to link poverty and "minority", viz., being lesser brethren, Marian poverty makes one lowly, like Mary (cf. the Magnificat, Lk. 1, 48), because placing one in a state of "minority", or being child of Mary[5].

So much for the distinctive mark of the Franciscan Order as seen first in St. Francis. But it is also important, indeed more important, to grasp the specific Marian feature of that mark. And if there is one privilege of Mary particularly associated

---

[5] On the essentially Marian character of the Rule of St. Clare, and by implication that of St. Francis of Assisi. cf. the interesting and well documented articles of the Poor Clares of the proto-monastery of Assisi: *La Regola di santa Chiara, una "sequela Christi" con Maria*, in *L'Osservatore Romano* (21 Nov., 2003) p. 7; and G. Cavazos-Gonzàlez, *Greater than a Mother's Love. Kinship in the Spirituality of Francis and Clare of Assisi* (Rome 2001).

with the Franciscan Order, indeed because it was so intimately bound up with the spirituality of St. Francis, and which since the beginning of that Order the followers of St. Francis have regarded as the glory of their community, it is the Immaculate Conception. It is this privilege which explains the incomparably singular character of the mystery of Mary, the Mother of God: a mystery at the heart both of the *Salute to the Virgin* and the *Antiphon of the Office of the Passion* of St. Francis. This is the mystery whose solemn definition under that title in 1854 owes so much to the centuries long, uninterrupted efforts of all Franciscan families.

But this is also the mystery which, as St. Maximilian Kolbe points out (*SK* 1284; 1310; and competent scholarly studies confirm[6]), clearly is present in the life and writings of St. Francis under the title "Spouse of the Holy Spirit" or "absolute Kingship or primacy of Jesus as Word Incarnate" or "presence of Mary in the counsels of the Father as his first-born daughter chosen *ante omnia saecula*, consecrated by the Three Divine Persons to be Mother of the Son"[7], who was not, like us "culpable of the crucifixion of her Son", and yet did not hesitate to sacrifice that Son willingly for our salvation, for the possibility of our sharing in His life, death, and resurrection. All of this identifies concretely what Bl. John Duns Scotus means by being redeemed "preservatively", or what Vatican II means by being redeemed preeminently, and thereby constituted preeminent member of the Church, her figure and mother. She is the

---

[6] Cf. Schneider, *op. cit.*, pp. 176-177; 220-233, in particular 232-233; see also P. D. Fehlner, "Una tesi di San Massimiliano su San Francesco e l'Immacolata alla luce della ricerca recente," in *Miles Immaculatae* 20 (1984) 165-186.

[7] In the writings of St. Francis: Ps. 15 of the *Office of the Passion*, to be related with the *Regula non bullata* 23, 1-3, and *Admonition* 5, 1-3 (We crucified Him, Mary did not, by sin, where original sin is primarily intended). Addressing Mary as tabernacle of the Word Incarnate is a clear allusion to Ecclesiasticus 24, 12 (vulgate) where Mary (Immaculate) is understood to be the tabernacle of the Word *Incarnate* in the eternal counsels of God. Whence, the traditional scotistic reading of St. Paul in Ephesians 1, 1 ff., and Col. 1, 13 ff. as a basis for the scotistic thesis on absolute primacy of Christ and Mary.

Queen of the *Portiuncula*, of our human family as well as of the Angels, the Esther for love of whom the King gave His life to save her Mardochaeus-Francis, viz., the rest of her people, the "poor of Yahweh"[8].

All this has a crucial bearing on how the form of life which Christ gave to St. Francis in answer to his prayer for vocational enlightenment: illumination of the darkness of his heart with wisdom and understanding (*Oratio ante crucifixum* dicta)[9], viz., perfect conformity in soul and body to the Crucified who answered his prayer from the crucifix in San Damiano, and the task for which this was given in the Church, are to be understood. Our Crucified Lord, speaking to St. Francis from the icon of the Cross in San Damiano asked him to "repair His Church: do you not see that it is falling into ruin?"

We are not in the habit of noticing the other figures in that eastern, Syriac style icon: Our Lady, St. John, the other "Mary's" and the Roman soldiers, and a host of angels and saints, or their arrangement[10]. I shall return to this important remark later. Here I wish to stress one thing only, one which should make my essay relatively easy to follow. Mary in the crucifix of San Damiano is clearly depicted as the Woman of Genesis and of the Apocalypse, on Calvary the Coredemptress because maternal Mediatress to whom the one Mediator entrusts, in the person of John, all the redeemed. On this presence of Mary rests the formation and repair of the Church.

And in the vocation of Francis and of his followers that Woman is maternal *Mediatress* of all graces: Mother *of* and *in* the Church, because she is the *Immaculate Conception*. The history of Franciscanism, beginning with St. Francis, is an anticipation and preparation for what Our Lady said in reply to the question of St. Bernadette (and the question of all

---

[8] St. Bonaventure, *Apologia Pauperum*, 11.
[9] Cf. Schneider, *op. cit.*, pp. 33 ff.
[10] *Ibid.*, pp. 8 ff.; 21 ff.

of us: *who* are you, what does your person mean? – Cf. St. Maximilian, *SK* 1305, 1317, 1318): *I am the Immaculate Conception*. The younger contemporaries and first genera- tions of Francis' followers implicitly grasped this when they described his and their spirituality in terms of the maternal mediation of Mary in the mystery of the Church: She is our Mediatress with Christ as Christ is our Mediator with the Father: Henry of Avranche, whose assessment of the essential character of St. Francis' spirituality and theology of the heart is reflected in the major theme of St. Bonaventure's mariolo- gy: universal Marian mediation[11].

The Immaculate Conception is that Marian mystery (priv- ilege in the sense of singular personal quality making possible our participation in her glory) which characterizes the inner- most sanctity of the Church: that fellowship, communion of persons, linking the Church to her Head as bride to groom (cf. 1 Jn. 1, 3: Eph. 5, 27). St. Paul tells us Christ gave His life, shed His blood, that the Church might be cleansed (liberative redemption) from sin, without spot (*sine macula*) in soul, with- out blemish or wrinkle (*sine ruga*) in body, like His Virgin Mother, "preeminent member" of the Church, because Mother of the Church. (cf. Eph. 5, 27). This is the key to the "mystery of His will" (Eph. 1, 9), that reason of the divine heart, which brings heaven to earth and earth to heaven.

The faith of Mary, which is the faith of the Church, is a blessed faith, not merely to analyze intellectually, not merely to cultivate devotionally, but to contemplate as point of departure

---

[11] "Mediatrix Virgo beata ad Christum, Christus ad Patrem sit Mediator": Henry of Avranches, *Legenda versificata S. Francisci*, in *Analecta Franciscana* X (Quaracchi 1926, 1941) 405-491, here 448; "(Maria) Mediatrix est inter nos et Christum, sicut Christus inter nos et Deum": St. Bonaventure, III *Sent.*, d. 3, p. 1, a. 1, q. 2; "Sicut et Deus nos venit per ipsam (Mariam), ita per ipsam nos oportet redire in Deum": St. Bonaventure, *Commentarium in Lucam* 1, 70. The context of this last citation makes it expressly clear, that according to the Seraphic Doctor by divine disposition no one passes the gate of heaven without the mediation of Mary. This is the central meaning of her title "Gate of heaven": for us to pass to heaven, as it is for God to pass to earth.

for attaining blessed life: beatitude, here and hereafter. "Blessed is she who has believed, because the things spoken to her shall be accomplished". The foundation of Mary's *Fiat*, matching and complementing as St. Anselm says (*Oratio* 52, second lesson for the office of readings of the solemnity of the Immaculate Conception) the *Fiat* of Father and Son, is that faith, and the heart of that living faith is the Immaculate Conception. That mystery makes possible her cooperation centered essentially in her *Fiat* matching perfectly the primary *Fiat* of the counsels of the Father's will to create and save, and through her therefore every form of our collaboration, again centered in and arising out of a *Fiat* "transubstantiated"[12] by her maternal mediation and according to her maternal exemplar.

The maximal fruit of her human *fiat* or of any human *fiat* is Jesus, the incarnation of the Word for the redemption of mankind, fruit of her womb. So every Christian by grace is, according to St. Francis, an extension of Mary for the conception and birth of Jesus spiritually in the minds and hearts of all whom Christ redeemed (cf. St. Francis, *Letter to the Faithful II*, 48-53). Without her *fiat* and maternal intervention in our lives, no activity on our part in the economy of salvation, viz., the supernatural order, is possible; or at best the sterile *fides sola* of Luther, which is simply a pious way of affirming the principle of all secularism: supernatural works, divine-like works on our part are by definition impossible, even for God.

But we may see in the Lutheran exclusion of Marian mediation a kind of confirmation of the Catholic position based on the mystery of the Immaculate Conception: all cooperation in the work of salvation hinges on the mystery of Mary or it is impossible. Hence, from the repudiation of the maternal mediation of Mary resting ultimately on the mystery of the Immaculate Conception at the time of the renais-

---

[12] A favorite phrase of St. Maximilian Ma. Kolbe: cf. *SK* 508. Cf. also the recent study of Fr. Angelo M. Geiger, F.I., "Marian Mediation as Presence and Transubstantiation into the Immaculate," in *Mary at the Foot of the Cross III* (New Bedford, MA: Franciscans of the Immaculate, 2003) 127-171.

sance, reformation, and secularization in the West stems the crisis of faith we are now undergoing.

Whence, we can see how important is the question of the Immaculate Conception in determining what answer is given to the question: are good works, is merit, is cooperation in the work of salvation possible in theory? While no creature can cooperate in a strictly creative work, a creature can cooperate in a strictly salvific work, as St. Anselm, and after him all the great scholastics, in the above cited *Oratio 52* notes. That possibility rests on and is revealed in the person of Mary, the Immaculate Conception, and is made possible for all through Mary, both in her cooperation at the start of the Incarnation as His Mother, in the supreme work of the Incarnate Word (redemptive sacrifice of Calvary) as His Coredemptress, and in the realization of His triumph in the glorification of the Church as mediatress of all graces (triumph of the Kingdom as triumph of the Immaculate Heart).

In the light of these considerations I intend to treat the three points of the title of my essay, beginning with the last: 1) the present crisis or ruining of the Church, what it has in common with the same in the days of St. Francis, or failure to take account of the Immaculate Conception in the "faith" of the Church and of Christians, and what is the core of renewal or repair; 2) the Immaculate in the life and work of St. Francis; 3) the *Salute* to the Immaculate or Virgin consecrated from all eternity by Father, Son, and Holy Spirit as key form of total consecration or true devotion, indispensable basis for repair of the Church as well as key to the new evangelization and resolution to the ecumenical question.

I.   The Church falling into ruin, or Crisis of Faith.

Some may think this too harsh a statement, one suggesting, not too delicately, that the Church is not securely anchored on the Rock, and that perhaps the radical critics of

Vatican II, both left and right, for different reasons, of course, nonetheless are correct in their conclusion: the Council was a failure, and responsible for the ever worsening condition of the Church.

Both are wrong, but that does not change the fact that the statement was made by Christ Himself, that it was true in 1206 and it is still true today. What does it really mean?

The fact that the Church will not be destroyed, that it will remain securely founded on Rock (Christ principally, but visibly in the Church militant the successor of St. Peter) rather than sand (cf. Mt. 7, 25; 16, 18) does not change the fact that there is a crisis to be dealt with and a renewal of faith to be undertaken in view of a very concrete goal: that the Church, in the words of St. Paul, might be *sine macula et sine ruga*, viz., fully like her exemplar, the Immaculate Virgin Mother (cf. Eph. 5, 27). In other words we are speaking of the realization of the full implications of the Immaculate Conception in the words of St. Francis: *Virgo Ecclesia facta*. To the saintly children at Fatima, Our Lord as well as Our Lady made it quite clear that the goal of all prayer and penance and reparation is the triumph of the Immaculate Heart, the full glorification of the Church in the sanctification and salvation of her every member.

The crisis in question is what is known today as the crisis of faith: not in terms of the object of belief, as though it might be dubious, as every kind of skeptic would have us "believe," or that the foundations of the Church are insecure, but in the sense that so many professed believers are unsure of what they believe, or no longer have any firm determination to live what they believe fully, whether this lack of conviction touch the private or the communal aspects of Christian discipleship.

How can the heart of this crisis be identified, convincingly yet without excessively long and tiring analysis? St.

Maximilian Ma. Kolbe, one of the outstanding disciples of St. Francis in our times, called Patron of our trouble times by the Pope who canonized him in 1982, has perhaps best identified the heart of that crisis of faith in terms of the Immaculate Conception. The solemn definition of the Immaculate Conception in 1854, he says (*SK* 1486), signaled the end of what seemed to contemporary observers a slide of the Church toward non-existence. Without the slightest doubt, that solemn act of homage to the Mother of God accounts for the Church's rapid renewal despite the loss of the Papal States, the general secularization in Europe, the modernist crisis, the First World War, a renewal evident to all. In theology that renewal revolved about the key question of the maternal mediation of Mary in the Church. What was accomplished within living memory, was but a more spectacular illustration of the driving force behind the counter-reformation in Catholic Europe: the mediation of the Immaculate. This mystery was the exact counter-point to the Protestant war-cry: *solus Christus* affirmed precisely in the repudiation of Marian mediation (and therefore ecclesial-hierarchical-sacramental in all forms) resting on Mary's pre-eminent mode of redemption, viz., preservative, "from all taint of original sin" (even of the so-called *debitum peccati* according to scotistic tradition), enabling her to be Mother of God and Mother of the Church.

Now, the fact that Our Lady's mediation is always victorious does not mean that the victory is realized in a single instant. Anyone who has pondered Rev. 12, especially as the fulfillment of the prophecy of Gen. 3, 15 (a prophecy whose possibility is related to the typology of Adam and Eve revealed before the fall in relation to Christ and Mary – cf. Gen. 2, 20 ff. and the commentaries of Sts. Bonaventure and Thomas), an all-inclusive vision of the divine counsels of salvation (cf. Eph. 1, 1 ff.) in the course of realization, will perceive the justice of St. Bonaventure's comment on the theology of history: all history is governed by the incessant conflict between the Christ and His Church on the one hand, and on the other the anti-christ (or devil) and his anti-church (the two cities of St. Augustine): *Collationes in Hexaemeron*, c 14, n. 17. In this contest, as it appears in the works of the great Franciscan Doctor, the Woman of Genesis, of Bethlehem and Calvary, of heavenly glory, occupies the point where the two opposed forces meet. To grasp this quickly and effectively, we need only recall the prophecy of Simeon during the Purification-Presentation of Jesus and Mary for the sake of the Church: the sword of sorrow will pierce your soul, that the thoughts of many might be revealed (cf. Lk. 2, 35) and its fulfillment on Calvary (Jn. 19, 25-27), so profoundly expounded by the Seraphic Doctor, especially in his *Collationes de septem donis Spiritus Sancti*, c. 6, and in his *Sermones* for the feasts of the Nativity, Annunciation, Purification, and Assumption of the Blessed Virgin[13].

The division between belief and unbelief, between fidelity and infidelity, so clearly indicated by St. Francis in his praises of the Virgin, passes through the Immaculate. For this, above all in the aforementioned *Salute to the Virgin*, St. Francis begs his Advocate-Paraclete (cf. *2 Cel.* 198; St. Bonaventure, *Leg. Major*, 9, 1) to intervene (note: not only to intercede as the other saints, but directly intervene, because and therefore as only Coredemptress, redeemed not *liberative* like the rest of the saints after the fact of the redemption accomplished, but *preservative*, viz., in a pre-eminent way, because participant under and with her Son in the initiation of that work at His conception and birth and in its very

---

[13] Cf. P. D. Fehlner, "The Sense of Marian Coredemption in St. Bonaventure and Bl. John Duns Scotus", in *Mary at the Foot of the Cross I* (New Bedford, MA: Franciscans of the Immaculate, 2001) 103-118; IDEM, "Il Mistero della Corredenzione secondo il Dottore Serafico San Bonaventura", in *Maria Corredentrice. Storia e Teologia II* (Frigento 1999) pp. 11-91; IDEM, "Immaculata Mediatrix – Toward a Dogmatic Definition of the Coredemption", in *Mary Coredemptrix, Mediatrix, Advocate. Theological Foundations II*, ed. M. Miravalle (Santa Barbara, CA: Queenship, 1996) pp. 259-329.

accomplishment on Calvary): with all the heavenly forces at her disposal in the hearts of men, so that from being unfaithful they might become faithful.

This intervention in terms of faith, so clearly pinpointed by St. Francis in terms of the Church as temple of her Savior Head recalls the faith of Mary whereby she first conceived in her heart by faith Him whom she later conceived by the power of the Holy Spirit in her body. It further recalls the victory of faith over the "liar and murderer" from the beginning (cf. Jn. 8, 44), a victory in which the Woman of Genesis 3, 15 plays the key role of *Mater et Magistra*, as the Church in the liturgy has always recognized: *Thou hast destroyed all heresies in the entire world*. Mary is, in the words of St. Bonaventure, *Magistra Apostolorum*[14], because she is Mother of God. We may add with Bl. John Duns Scotus, crossing the i's and dotting the t's of St. Francis, Mother because Immaculate, Spouse of the Holy Spirit.

We must not, then, imagine that ecclesial crises occur abruptly, are primarily the result of wicked conspiracies of modernists, or narrow-minded governance by crusty old traditionalists. The potential for ruin, for subtle and impressive manipulation of all shades of ideological inclination in the Church by the prince of this world is always possible, and not only possible. It is no doubt regularly in the process of being activated, it being relatively easy for one to stir the pot towards boiling point who knows the secret of the Church's security, the Woman whose heel the serpent fears, and can distract the attention of the faithful from her. But it is even easier to control and

---

[14] Cf. P. Fehlner, *Mater et Magistra Apostolorum*, in *Immaculata Mediatrix* 1 (1/2001) 15-95. Cf. also C. Schönborn, *Maria – Herz der Theologie – Theologie des Herzens*, in *Weisheit Gottes – Weisheit der Welt, I* (Erzabtei St. Ottilien 1987) 575-598; F. Léthel, *Connaître l'amour qui surpasse toute connaisance. La Théologie des Saints* (Venasque 1989), and by the same *Il linguaggio mistico di San Massimiliano Maria Kolbe*, in *Miles Immaculatae* 38 (2002) 763-797; P. Fehlner, *Scientia et Pietas*, in *Immaculata Mediatrix* 1 (3/2001) 11-48, and his *Io sono l'Immacolata Concezione. Adhuc quaedam de metaphysica mariana*, in *Immaculata Mediatrix* 2 (2002) 15-41.

blunt that manipulation if those who love and guide the Church know that mystery of the Immaculate Conception better.

That role of the Marian mystery in the Church has recently been underscored by Pope John Paul II in *Redemptoris Mater* (and in much of the rest of his Marian writing as Pope) in terms of Marian presence: Mary is the memory of the Church. When the Church can be persuaded to ignore, downplay, minimalize that dynamic presence, then the factors contributing to her ruin can be activated, take on a primary role in the midst of so many other positive factors, thereby not only preventing the attainment of victory, but producing impressive phenomena of decay, touching not only the works of the apostolate and externals of Church order, but striking at the very life of faith and sacramental practice.

We may say, then, given what some (including the present successor of St. Peter – see, e.g., *Redemptoris Mater*) have called the Marian personality of the Church[15], a crisis of faith is radically a Marian crisis, not of Mary, but of lack of due devotion to Mary, absence of that unconditional, limitless character of "true devotion", "Marian slavery," "total possession" by Mary, in the words of the present Pope's coat of arms: *Totus Tuus*. Marianization of our faith means not simply additional devotional exercises, or additional study of Marian dogmas, but a total marianization of the structures of Christian existence, personal and communal.

St. Maximilian (cf. *SK* 485; 486) anticipated all this in observing that the solemn definition of the Immaculate Conception was not simply the final triumph of Mary and of the Church, but a key step leading to what he called the incorporation of the mystery of the Immaculate into the life of the Church and of all mankind[16]. Without this the Church would be

---

[15] Cf. the detailed overview and analysis of Fr. J. Ferrer Arellano, "Marian Coredemption and Sacramental Mediation," in *Mary at the Foot of the Cross III* (New Bedford, MA: Franciscans of the Immaculate, 2003) 70-126.

[16] For a fuller exposition of the Kolbean theology of history cf. P. Fehlner, "The Other Page", in *Miles Immaculatae* 24 (1988) 512-531.

subject to the forces of ruin. Only on this basis could the work of repair – reparation – be undertaken successfully. It was precisely the failure before the Council to accomplish this incorporation, viz., to marianize every aspect of the life of faith, including theology and philosophy, which made the Council necessary, but which also made the results of the Council so far inconclusive at best.

History bears out the analysis of St. Maximilian. The Council of Trent was a great Council, but few remember it took not only decades, but centuries to realize securely what the counter-reformation had in mind: salvation of the Church from subversion threatened by the new piety purified of Mary: *solus Christus* and therefore *sola fides* and not good works as the basis of justification and the supernatural. That goal was only effectively achieved with the solemn definition of 1854, filling a lacuna of the Council over the Immaculate Conception. The maculists would have condemned the dogma; the immaculatists (led by the Franciscan scotists) were not strong enough to secure a definition, and so the compromise: the decree on the universality of original sin was declared not to touch Mary. But if the compromise did not touch doctrinal truth and achieved relative peace within the Church, the failure to fully honor the Mother of the Church allowed the Protestant reform to solidify and eventually prepare the way for the enlightenment (secularism), the revolution and the modernism-traditionalism split fueling our present crisis of faith. A similar struggle and compromise over Mary at Vatican II, this time over a corollary of the Immaculate Conception, viz., the coredemption and universal mediation, this one more public, occurred. It is not unreasonable to see this failure, rather than any teaching of the Council, as reason for the relative sterility of the post-conciliar aftermath.

On this, too, St. Maximilian's analysis is prophetic. According to St. Maximilian repair (including restoration) of the Church, perfect conformation to Christ Crucified, ultimate goal of Tridentine reform, in a sense the radical goal taken up again by Vatican II and the true meaning of a much debated cliché, *aggiornamento*, is attained by incorporating the mystery of the Immaculate into life, above all the life of faith. By this he means not only faith as intellectual assent or affective obedience, but as the distinctive feature of a way of life in response to the grace of justification and sanctification. It is this Marian response – commonly called today total consecration to the Immaculate – which stands at the heart of St. Francis' work, reparation of the Church, and which in his day significantly contributed to the postponement of the Protestant reformation (and its sequel – secularization) for three centuries, until via the mystery of the Immaculate Conception the Church would be better able to deal with that and subsequent crises.

Once we recall that the source of Francis' grace of vocation was Christ Himself (cf. *Testament*, 4; *Oratio ante crucifixum* dicta), and realize that Christ's desire expressed in the Fatima messages for the triumph of the Immaculate Heart is but an amplification of the message of the Crucified from the cross in San Damiano, then the significance of the Franciscan Marian phenomenon in the Church and for the Church stands out in all its importance. Enlightenment of the darkness of our hearts, as for Francis of Assisi before the Crucifix of San Damiano and throughout his life, comes only via the mediation of the *Immaculate Coredemptress* and is carried forward under her guidance as *Mater et Magistra*, who kept all those mysteries in her heart, pondering them (cf. Lk 2, 19. 51). This is the central message of Francis to the Church of his and our day.

II.   St. Francis and the Immaculate Conception

Much scholarly research in the years just before the Council, during the Council and since, has been devoted to a study of the Marian dimension of St. Francis' life and work. The general conclusion is this: that the life and work of the Poverello is essentially Marian, that it has no other reason to be except as a service to Mary, a service sought by her and guaranteed by her[17]. These conclusions confirm the estimate of the Order common to all Franciscan generations and families up to about a century or less ago. Within the context of such an estimate, the totally Marian character of St. Maximilian's life and work appears fully traditional, connatural, and logical, something so much to be expected that its not-occurring would have been the major surprise and shock of Franciscan history.

In a very recent article in *L'Osservatore Romano* in preparation for the solemnity of the Immaculate Conception, 2003, Archbishop Angelo Amato, Secretary of the Congregation for the Doctrine of the Faith, makes just this point: the Franciscan tradition, specifically the scotistic thesis on the reason for the Immaculate Conception and the primacy of Christ, with the solemn definition of 1854, no longer was a mere "*opinio minorum*", but entered the mainstream of Catholic doctrine, to be renewed by many figures of the contemporary Church, above all in extraordinary fashion by the martyr of charity, St. Maximilian Ma. Kolbe[18].

That so many of his contemporary Franciscans should have seen St. Maximilian as a Franciscan eccentric, and that today a majority of those professing to be Franciscan should

---

[17] For detailed analysis of these studies cf. Schneider, *op. cit.*, pp. xxvi ff., and 355-376.

[18] A. Amato, "Criterio formativo della 'Milizia' fondata da S. Massimiliano Kolbe", in *L'Osservatore Romano*, 7 Dec., 2003, p. 11. The "opinion" of Scotus in question is the distinction between preservative and liberative redemption within the definition of most perfect redemption and the bearing of this thesis on the absolute primacy of Christ. On the overall significance of the Franciscan-scotistic tradition for the key mariological issues central to all contemporary theology cf. P. Fehlner, "Immaculata Mediatrix – Toward a Dogmatic Definition of the Coredemption", in *Mary Coredemptrix, Mediatrix, Advocate. Theological Foundations II*, ed. M. Miravalle (Santa Barbara, CA: Queenship, 1996) 259-329.

no longer think of their Order as essentially Marian is indeed a major surprise, shock, and tragedy[19].

But once we become aware of the key features of that Marian tradition which is the Franciscan Order, indeed has its conscious origins in the Seraphic Patriarch himself, then we will be able to appreciate the conclusions of those scholars who maintain that even if the title *Immaculate Conception* does not appear in any of the writings of St. Francis, the reality is clearly present. Examining these, in particular the *Salute to the Virgin* and the *Antiphon* for the *Office of the Passion*, we shall realize that far from being a scholastic-scotistic abstraction, the Immaculate Conception as a title is biblically rooted and denotes a content, not only negative – no sin, but profoundly positive – all grace. That positive aspect is made clear in the manner in which St. Francis, and so many Franciscan saints after him, conceive the relations of the Immaculate Virgin to the Three Divine Persons, a mode of Trinitarian meditation stressed in the Marian catechesis of the present Pope, one reflecting Mary's mode of reflection noted by the Poverello: keeping all these mysteries in her heart, pondering them (Lk 2, 19. 51).

1.   The *Salute to the Virgin*

First the text, in the original Latin, without which it is difficult to appreciate the profound, yet simply and limpidly clear nuances of the Saint.

Ave Domina, sancta Regina,	Hail Lady, holy Queen,
sancta Dei genetrix Maria,	holy Mary, Mother of God,
quae es virgo ecclesia facta	who art virgin made church
et electa a sanctissimo	chosen by the most holy
Patre de caelo,	Father in heaven
quam consecravit cum	whom with
sanctissimo dilecto Filio suo	his most holy beloved Son

---

[19] Cf. Schneider, *op. cit.*, p. xxvii and note 7.

et Spiritu Sancto Paraclito,	and the Holy Spirit Paraclete,
in qua fuit et est omnis plenitu-	in whom was and is all fullness
do gratiae et omne bonum.	of grace and every good.
Ave palatium eius;	Hail, his palace;
Ave tabernaculum eius;	Hail, his tabernacle;
Ave domus eius;	Hail, his house;
Ave vestimentum eius;	Hail, his vestment;
Ave ancilla eius;	Hail, his handmaid;
Ave mater eius;	Hail, his mother;
et vos omnes sanctae virtutes,	and all you holy virtues,
quae per gratiam et illumina-	which by grace and by the illu-
tionem Spiritus Sancti	mination of the Holy Spirit
infundimini in corda fidelium,	are poured into the hearts of the
ut de infidelibus fideles Deo	faithful,
faciatis.	that from being unfaithful they
	might become faithful to God.

That the *Salute* has as its context the mystery of the Church as temple or house of God is quite obvious, not only from the verse *Virgo Ecclesia facta*, but from the numerous references to our Lady as palace, tabernacle, abode, vestment: hence handmaid and mother, and to her maternal intercessory intervention in the lives of believers, that they might fully realize the life of faith. Hence, the origin of the *Salute* is in close relation, historically and theologically, with Francis's mystical experience in 1206 before the Crucifix of San Damiano, and his subsequent association with St. Mary of the Angels (said to have been chanted there by Francis for the anniversary of dedication, August 2, in preparation for the feast of the Assumption)[20]. Whence, the precise identifi-

---

[20] On the devotion of St. Francis to this little Marian sanctuary cf. *1 Celano.* 21 *2 Celano.* 19; St. Bonaventure, *Legenda Major* 3, 1; *Legend of the Three Companions* 6. This link between the *Salute*, Francis' mystical experience at San Damiano, and St. Mary of the Angels most probably is reflected in the Seraphic Doctor's stupendous sermons on the Assumption of Our Lady with their Marian ecclesiology. Cf. P. D. Fehlner, *The Role of Charity in the Ecclesiology of St. Bonaventure* (Rome 1965) pp. 74-95. Here can be perceived the very ancient tradition

cation of the person of the Mother of God, Lady and Queen, as "consecrated" and therefore full of grace and "all Good", hence able to mediate holiness for us, is crucial to an understanding of what constitutes the essential Marian character of St. Francis' spirituality and devotion to Christ and to the Church.

The Mother of God is the Virgin made Church (exemplar, figure, model of the Church in the language of Vatican II, *Lumen Gentium*, ch. 8 and *passim*; in another reading *Virgo perpetua*, which is the same mystery, for the perpetual virginity of Mary culminates in the mystery of the Church), chosen by the heavenly Father and so consecrated by Him together with Son and Holy Spirit, therefore in whom there was and always is the fullness of grace and "all good", that is the Incarnate Word, and so His palace, etc., and our Mediatress.

The decisive factor in the *Salute* for claiming St. Francis' vocation to repair the Church, to support it (as in the dream of Innocent III) rests on the mystery of the Immaculate Conception and is realized to the degree that mystery is lived in the Church are the phrases "chosen by the Father", and "consecrated by the Father", hence full of grace and all Good (viz., God Himself Incarnate).

Fr. Schneider has shown[21] that St. Francis in his writings, when speaking of Mary's election by the Father, consistently understands that election just as Scotus does, just as St. Maximilian does: "Who are you, O Immaculate? . . . not only creature, not only saint, but true Mother of God . . . in you alone God has been adored without compare more than in all the saints. For you alone God created the whole world, for you God called me into existence; whence this good fortune of mine?" (*SK* 1305; see also *SK* 1310: the Immaculate and the Trinity; *SK* 1311: the Immaculate and the trial of the Angels; and *SK* 1320, a recapitulation): as prior to the deci-

---

for a crucial point of the Marian ecclesiology of Vatican II, *Lumen Gentium*, ch. 8, whose title is "The Virgin Mary in the Mystery of Christ and of the Church."

[21] Cf. Schneider, *op. cit.*, pp. 170-184, in particular 183-184.

sion to create the universe: *ante omnia saecula* as in the traditional Franciscan reading of Proverbs 8 and Ecclesiasticus 24, hence making the creation of the universe dependent on the election of Mary to be Mother of God[22].

Her consecration, consequently, must be understood as beyond further perfection. Were we to borrow St. Anselm's famous dictum (in his work *On the Conception of the Virgin*, 18), we should say that in no possibly more perfect world could the consecration (or original holiness) of Mary be greater than it in fact is, transcending in virtue of the Immaculate Conception both the holiness of any other individual saint or of all the saints together considered apart from Mary[23]. In a word,

---

[22] For texts of St. Francis and studies on them cf. Schneider, *op. cit.*, pp. 183-184. On Scotus there is a relatively extensive bibliography available in English on the absolute primacy of Christ (in St. Francis, absolute kingship): cf. J. Carol, *Why Jesus Christ? Thomistic, Scotistic and Conciliatory Perspectives* (Manasses, VA 1986), and on the joint predestination of Jesus and Mary, appearing in the bull *Ineffabilis Deus* (1854), dogmatic definition of the Immaculate Conception under the Latin form *uno eodemque decreto praedestonatus*, and again in *Munificentissimus Deus* (1950) for the definition of the Assumption. The key role ascribed to the "preexistence" of Mary Immaculate as part of that first "sign" of the divine salvific will of the Father in the pontifical Magisterium (and conciliar of Vatican II citing this very notion of joint predestination) underscores the importance of the Franciscan-scotistic analysis of the *signa voluntatis divinae* and their order as basis of the possility and intelligibility of anything contingent and created. On this point there is very little available in English. One might begin serious research on the metaphysical questions involved studying two works in German: W. Hoeres, *Die Wille als reine Vollkommenheit nach Duns Scotus* (Munich 1962); and H.-J. Werner, *Die Ermöglichung des endlichen Seins nach Johannes Duns Scotus* (Bern-Frankfurt 1974). In the context of such studies a number of observations of the Jesuit poet Fr. Gerard M. Hopkins on the "preexistence of Mary and the Word as Incarnate" (not the real preexistence of the Word as Word) in the mind of God appear as especially profound. Cf. G. M. Hopkins, *The Sermons and Devotional Writings of Gerard Manley Hopkins*, ed. by C. Devlin, SJ (London 1959) *passim* (cf. index).
[23] St. Bonaventure clearly affirms this, e.g. *Sermo V* on the Assumption: "Quidquid enim dignitatis et gloriae istis (sanctis) partialiter est collatum, sacrae Virgini integraliter est concessum", and therefore (in sermon I on the Assumption) whatever of grace is in all other saints and angels derives

she is without any trace of original sin, not even the so-called *debitum*[24], because on her joint predestination with Christ depends the predestination of Adam and Eve. She is solely under the headship of Christ. Whence her redemption is preservative, not liberative, and therefore she can actively contribute to our liberation as Mother of God and Coredemptress.

Or in the words of St. Francis, she alone is not guilty of the crucifixion and so can merit by her compassion for us, making it possible for us in fact to actively collaborate in filling up for the Church what is lacking to the sufferings of Christ (subjective redemption: cf. St. Paul, Col. 1, 24). Another word for this is Immaculate Conception: all grace, no sin; total unity of wills of Creator and creature, of their respective *Fiat* in view of the Incarnation (all good) and the attainment of the maximum glory of God in the sanctification of the Church. This is what is meant by repair of the Church so as to be without spot or wrinkle, or to incorporate the mystery of the Immaculate Conception into the Church.

As we shall now see, this Marian mystery of the Immaculate Conception, or the primordial consecration of Mary before all ages, is defined more precisely in the *Antiphon* of the *Office of the Passion* in what today would be described as the terminology of Trinitarian theology.

2.   The *Antiphon* of the *Office of the Passion*

First the text in Latin, arranged in order to make clear its triadic literary structure so appropriate to the mystery of Mary, Church, and salvation in relation to the Triune Godhead.

---

from and through her (Mary). The influence of St. Francis and his devotion to Our Lady of the Angels, viz., the Assumption, is perfectly obvious. Cf. Fehlner, *The Role of Charity . . .* cit., pp. 74-90.

[24] For the history of controversy and bibliography cf. J. Carol, ofm, *A History of the Controversy over the "Debitum Peccati"* (St. Bonaventure, NY: Franciscan Institute, 1978).

Sancta Maria Virgo	Holy Virgin Mary
non est tibi similis nata	there is none like you born
in mundo in mulieribus,	in the world among women
filia et ancilla	daughter and handmaid
altissimi summi	of the most high supreme
Regis Patris	Father King
caelestis,	in heaven
mater	Mother
sanctissimi Domini nostri	of our most holy Lord
Jesu Christi,	Jesus Christ,
sponsa	Spouse
Spiritus Sancti	of the Holy Spirit:
ora pro nobis	pray for us
cum	With
Sancto Michaele archangelo	St. Michael the archangel
et omnibus virtutibus caelorum	and all the virtues of heaven
et omnibus sanctis	and all the saints
apud	in the company of
tuum sanctissimum dilectum	your most holy beloved
Filium Dominum et Magistrum.	Son, Lord and Master

The *Antiphon*, like the *Salute*, is to be numbered among the oldest of St. Francis' writings, known to have been used by St. Clare as early as 1212. Without a doubt, its inspiration is drawn from the mystical experience of 1206, and with the *Salute* helps us to understand the "indescribable praise and devotion" (*2 Cel.* 200; St. Bonaventure, *Leg. Major* 7, 1) which St. Francis showered on Our Lady "because she made accessible to us as brother the Lord of majesty" (*2 Cel.* 198)[25], and "gave to Him His poverty and frailty" (*Letter to the Faithful II*, 4), that is, His capacity to suffer for our redemption. So, too, it helps us to grasp concretely what is his point of reference when he describes all the faithful, above all Franciscan tertiaries, as extensions of the maternal mediation of Mary in giving birth to Christ in the minds and

---

[25] A text clearly reflected in Bonaventure: *Sermo IV* on the Annunciation; cf. also *Sermo I* for Easter Monday.

hearts of others (*Letter to the Faithful II*, 48-53). But most of all it enables us to understand why perfect conformity to Christ crucified is only possible via perfect identification of self with the compassion of that Woman who is described in this work of inspiration: the Immaculate Coredemptress as Francis encountered her in the Crucifix of San Damiano.

The *Office of the Passion*, a devotional office composed by St. Francis, analogous to the *Little Office of the Blessed Virgin* which he recited; indeed, this office is a kind of adaptation of the *Little Office* to the central mystery of salvation, the sacrifice of Calvary. What is most significant about the Antiphon within the *Office of the Passion* is its role in nuancing the entire *Office* and experience of the Passion: it serves to frame all the psalms composed by the Saint in meditating on the biblical psalms in reference to the suffering and death of Jesus. It serves not only as the only antiphon for every hour of the office, but also as the only reading, responsorial, and prayer. In effect it reveals the Marian mode of the passion and death of Christ and therefore what we today call the coredemption. Just as the birth of the Savior is incomprehensible apart from the divine maternity of Mary, so neither is His saving death comprehensible apart from the Virgin's compassion, and therefore the fruits of that passion in the Church like the miracle of His birth of the Woman passes through the mystery of her virginal maternity and maternal virginity. She is the Virgin made Church. We are what we are as believers, the faith of the Church is what it is, indeed the Church is what she is because of what Mary is, the Immaculate Conception. This thought, so prominent in the Marian catechesis of the present Pope, and indeed in Vatican II, is a major theme in St. Bonaventure's sermons for the feast of the Assumption (unfortunately not available in English).

It is not wrong, therefore, to affirm that the personality of the Church is Marian, and no less a scholar than Jacques Maritain, in his last book[26], affirmed not only that, but that a

---

[26] J. Maritain, *L'Église: sa personne et son personnel* (Paris 1974): cf. Ferrer Arellano, *op. cit.*, pp. 73, 114, 122.

failure to realize and live accordingly stands at the root of the current crisis. God permits such crises that we might realize more clearly and be motivated more strongly to do what He wants accomplished: contribute to the triumph of the Immaculate Heart (in the language of Fatima), to the incorporation of the mystery of the Immaculate Coredemptress into the Church and all reality (dogmatic language of the Church).

One may wonder at the genius of Francis in theology, untutored as he was. But so did contemporary theologians who realized his thought soared like an eagle's, like that of the beloved disciple John, whom St. Bonaventure tells us was instructed in theology by Mary (cf. *2 Cel.* 103)[27]. There is indeed in the *Little Office* prayed by St. Francis a partial model, an antiphon dating around the 8th century and going like this:

> *Virgo Maria, non est tibi similis nata in mundo in mulieribus,*
> *flores ut rosa, odor ut lilium: ora pro nobis ad tuum Filium.*

But a quick comparison with the *Antiphon* of St. Francis will reveal immediately the originality of St. Francis precisely in that Trinitarian dimension revealing the real content of Mary's singular privilege known as the Immaculate Conception. As Fr. Schneider observes[28], St. Francis' style of meditation, the *cordis ruminatio* (cf. *2 Cel.* 102), as a kind of extension of that of Mary who kept all the mysteries in her heart, pondering them (cf. Lk. 2, 19. 51, where the mysteries are those of the birth of Jesus and His loss and finding in the temple, viz., His passion, death and resurrection), reveals the identity of his teacher, none other than the Woman to whom the Savior in the icon of San Damiano had entrusted John – and Francis (cf. the allusions to Mary in *Regula non bullata* 24, 2-3; *Admonition* 28, 3; *2 Cel* 135-139). Through Mary and in union with Mary (we call this Marian consecration), Francis not merely contemplates, but enters the crucifixion

---

[27] Schneider, *op. cit.*, pp. xxxii-xlvi.
[28] *Ibid.*, pp. 125 ff.

scene exactly where the beloved Disciple stands. Hence, through the Mother of Jesus, the Woman of Genesis, he receives in his heart the wounds of Jesus, eventually two years before his death (4 Oct., 1226, at St. Mary of the Angels) to appear visibly in the stigmatization on Mt. Alvernia (17 Sept., 1224) as confirmation and explanation of his vocation and its significance for the Church.

The Trinitarian aspect of the mystery of Mary surely is a part of the deposit of faith. But never before St. Francis was it formulated so concisely and so exactly as in this Antiphon. Nor have we before or since so profound an analysis of the election of Mary (in the eternal counsels of God), or of the nature of her consecration which follows on her singular and therefore primary election to be the Mother of God as here. The election and consecration here described are what subsequently have been solemnly defined as the Immaculate Conception and what have come to be recognized, with St. Maximilian Ma. Kolbe, as key to the mystery of grace in believers and in the Church. Whence, the supreme importance of incorporation of this mystery into the Church and life of every person, and the practice of total consecration or true devotion to the Immaculate as the divinely appointed way to full conformity with Christ crucified, or sharing in His victimhood.

In a word, in describing concretely the content of the mystery of the Immaculate Conception St. Francis has clearly affirmed the "Franciscan thesis" in theology commonly associated with the name of Scotus[29]: the absolute primacy or

---

[29] Critics of Scotus, as even a first reading of Carol, *Why Jesus Christ?*, cit., will reveal, insist that the position of Scotus is merely an *opinio minorum*, without any secure basis in the Creed or Scripture, since both mention only our redemption or salvation as motive of the Incarnation. Not true: the Creed mentions our salvation as proximate motive: *propter nostram salutem*, but to the maximum glory of the Word Incarnate as incarnate ascribes the character of remote or final motive. Last in execution, first in intention, runs the old axiom. Our salvation, as St. Bernardine notes, only came about because the Father had already absolutely decreed the Incarnation and divine Maternity. On such a credal criterion Scotus and the scotists are correct in

kingship of the Word *qua* Incarnate in terms of the joint pre-destination of the Word to be the Son of Mary and the Virgin Immaculate to be Mother of God, in the Latin of the Magisterium their predestination *uno eodemque decreto* (Bl. Pius IX, Ven. Pius XII; Vatican II).

We may now briefly examine the details of this stupendous formulation. Because of her unique consecration by the Father with the Son and Spirit, Mary is absolutely singular not only among all creatures, invisible as well as visible, but among women born in the world. Mary, our Lady and Queen, is incomparable to any creature, even other women, though they may be compared or likened to her (*relatio disquiparantiae* of Scotus or non-mutual relation[30]), because Mary enjoys by *grace* from all eternity what the Son of God enjoys by *nature*: filiation with the Father. In the inspired phrase of St. Francis, she is the first-born daughter (*filia*) of the Father, first-born, and so before all other creatures and all of creation: *ante omnia saecula*. In this way, as a modern disciple

---

their exegesis of such Pauline passages as Eph. 1, 1 ff., Col. 1, 13 ff., Heb 1, 1 ff., and johannine such as Jn. 1, 1 ss; 17 1 ff., and their anticipation in Genesis 2-3 and the sapiential literature (Prov. 8 and Ecclesi 24) as bearing not simply on the primacy of the Word in creation, but of the Word as Incarnate. The question of the testing of the Angels and of our first parents is a key question: if their trial in any way centered on acceptance or rejection of the Incarnation and divine Maternity and the fall consisted in the refusal to honor Christ and His Mother, then the scotistic position is a part of the deposit of faith. Many Fathers and Doctors of the Church have held this position, so closely related to the mystery of the Immaculate Conception, lastly but not leastly St. Maximilian Ma. Kolbe (SK 1311). Cf. B. Ullathorne, osb, *The Immaculate Conception* (New York: Benziger Bros., 1904) pp. 64-80; Carol, *Why Jesus Christ?*... cit., pp. 414-415; P. Fehlner, *St. Maximilian Pneumatologist*, p. 17, note 43 (in course of publication by Academy of the Immaculate, New Bedford, MA).

[30] On this and on Scotus' explanation of the hypostatic union and analogously the divine and spiritual maternity cf. P. Migliore, ofmconv, *La teoria scotista della dipendenza ipostatica. Esposizione e rilievi critici* (Rome 1950) ; S. Ragazzini, ofmconv, *La divina Maternità di Maria nel suo concetto teologico integrale* (Rome 1948 - Frigento, 2 ed. 1986) and IDEM, *Maria Vita dell'anima. Itinerario mariano alla Ss. Trinità* (Rome 1960-Frigento, 2 ed. 1986).

of Scotus, Fr. G. M. Hopkins, SJ, so clearly saw, she pre-exists in the will of God, or with Scotus, in the *signa voluntatis divinae*, what we might call the logic of the divine *decuit* which is the ultimate source of intelligibility and possibility of the contingent[31].

Now, it is the possibility of the Immaculate Conception, of there being a creature who by the grace of being first-born daughter of the Father transcends the fallibility and peccability of the first Adam (or moral solidarity with the first Adam and subjection to the "debt" of original sin) and which makes possible the Incarnation and in a second sign the Redemption.

Whence this grace of being first-born, first-beloved daughter? This grace is from her consecration by Father with Son and Holy Spirit. That consecration passes through the second title given her: handmaid, instrument of the Most High King and Father for the Incarnation of his only-begotten Son. Therefore, consecration as the Immaculate daughter is in view of the worth or merit of the Son, precisely to be His slave or handmaid in the fullest sense, viz., His Mother at birth and at death.

How shall this be? By the power of the Holy Spirit, described as espousal to the Holy Spirit, who is the definition of highest love, that of the Father and Son, a love petitioned for us by our Savior in His high-priestly prayer (Jn. 17, 23 ff.) and revealed and realized for us during the final address of the Savior to His Mother, this most singular Woman, just before He died (Jn. 19, 25-27), as it were his final response to that Woman's request of Him at Cana: they have no wine (Jn. 2, 4 ff.). In practice, to call Mary spouse of the Holy Spirit is to call her Immaculate Conception, or as St. Maximilian, glossing this antiphon of St. Francis says: Mary is the created Immaculate Conception, because the Holy Spirit is the uncreated Immaculate Conception (*SK* 1318). All creation, all of us included, were made for Mary Immaculate, St.

---

[31] Cf. note 9 for bibliographical detail.

Maximilian writes so beautifully (*SK* 1305), paraphrasing the sense of Scotus. Or with St. Bernardine of Siena, if the Father insisted so much on our redemption after original sin, it was because He wanted Mary so much as Mother of his Son, impossible without our redemption after the fall[32].

This is the heart of the supernatural order, making possible the Incarnation via a virginal conception-birth of God and making possible our rebirth to a life that is all grace and sinless, in St. Peter's classic definition a participation in the nature of the Triune God (cf. 2 Pet. 1, 4), or in that of S. John, fellowship (communion) with Father and Son (cf. 1 Jn. 1, 1 ff).

The terminology and legitimacy of total consecration to and through the Immaculate in order to be totally consecrated to and through Christ to the Father from whom all originates, whether in eternity or in time, rests ultimately on the truth of the Immaculate Conception: total exemption from even the faintest stain of original sin in virtue of the foreseen merits of the Redeemer, as total consecration of Mary by the Trinity to the Trinity before any other creature and as reason for the existence of all other creation. Even the Son in a sense was entrusted, consecrated to her by the Father for the sake of the Divine Maternity, or in the words of Scotus, for the sake of a most perfect fruit of a most perfect redemption by a most perfect Redeemer[33].

What gives this perfection the character of a *ne plus ultra* is the Immaculate Conception, which is why St. Thomas, in addition to the Incarnation calls the divine Maternity and our salvation "quasi-infinites", viz., realities

---

[32] "Maria namque sola per multa annorum milia antequam nasceretur, primo et principaliter Adam et Evam et totam eius posteritatem praeservavit in esse. . . Propter praecipuam reverentiam et singularissimam dilectionem, quam habebat ad Virginem praeservavit. . . De ipsa namque nasci debebat Filius Dei Jesus. . . quia non fuisset exorta Virgo, nec per consequens Christus sive Deus carnem non vestisset humanam": St. Bernardine of Siena, *Sermo VIII: De superadmirabili gratia et gloria Matris Dei*, in *Opera Omnia* (Quaracchi 1950-1965) Vol. II, p. 373.

[33] Cf. III *Sent.*, d. 3, q. 1.

which God himself could not improve, even in a world more perfect than the one he actually made.

III.   The *Salute*: Total Consecration as basis for the Renewal of the Church

This brings us once again to the general theme of our symposium in honor of the 150th anniversary of the dogmatic definition of the Immaculate Conception by Bl. Pius IX, December 8, 1854, in the bull, *Ineffabilis Deus*: what is the bearing of this dogma on the faith of the Church?

Surely very much in many ways. But above all and before all, particularly as the Church comes ever closer to that moment when her Savior will appear in all His glory and the Church will share that glory, as the form, or better scotistically, *formalitas* of glory: that glory which determines the structure of ecclesial existence in the state of incorruptibility, of perfect spiritualization of body as well as soul, of being without spot or wrinkle – all grace and no sin. Only as the mystery of the Immaculate Conception is incorporated into the Church and into the lives of all men living and still to be born or suffering in Purgatory can the crisis of faith be resolved and victory secured over the prince of this world, the enemy who hath sowed the chaff in the field of the Lord, who has rendered the "good earth" sterile and incapable of nurturing the seed of grace (cf. Mt. 13, 1-52). The good earth is good, only to the degree it is like Mary. Only as the earth that is human nature, that is human culture, is human civilization, is human piety is marianized, becomes by grace one with the consecrated Virgin Mother of God, the Immaculate Conception, can it produce abundant fruit of the seed sown in it.

That conditioning of the earth from which the first Adam, and therefore through Adam all men born of Eve, was formed is only by way of the true "Virgin Earth," the Immaculate, of which the "slime of the earth" or "virgin earth" is the type or figure according to the Fathers and great scholastics (a point almost totally forgotten in current theology). But not only from the virgin earth which is Mary, but actively by her as willing Mother the new Adam is formed as perfect Adam, and through her all born of water and the Holy Spirit are formed as children of God, because born of the Mother of God they share the same new humanity.

Total consecration to the Immaculate, possession by the Immaculate as her "portiuncula", being lesser, being little, being her children, being her "slaves" are all terms connoting the same profound reality defined by Pope Paul VI thus: to be fully Christian one must be fully Marian[34]. Once we have

---

[34] On the Franciscan origins of Marian "slavery" cf. the works of Fray Juan de los Angelos and Fray Melchor de Cetina in *Misticos Franciscanos Espagñoles*, vol. III (Madrid 1949): *Esclavitud Mariana* pp. 691-704; and *Exhortatión a la Devotión de la Virgen Madre de Dios* 725-820, with introductions to each by Fr. Juan Bautista Gomis, OFM. Both works date from the early 17th century, anticipating the "True Devotion" of St. Louis Grignion de Montfort by nearly 100 years, and originate in a Poor Clare Conceptionist context, that associated in the 17th century above all with the Ven. Mary of Ágreda, whose *Mystical City of God* has always been regarded within the Franciscan Order as one of the finest examples of scotistic Mariology in a contemplative key, and by Spanish scholars as one of the greatest works of a great century for Spanish Mariology. Cf. the recent volume 69 of *Estudios Marianos*: *La Madre Ágreda y la Mariología Española del Siglo XVII* (Salamanca 2003) and the very competent defense of the spiritual and theological merit of the Ven. Mary of Ágreda in the face of renewed charges that her visions are neither supernatural nor their scotistic mariology sound. Reference is often made, e.g., by St. Maximilian Ma. Kolbe, to a saying of St. Francis preserved in the older editions (up to about a century ago) of the *Fioretti of St. Francis*, that he wished his sons always to be faithful servants (or slaves) of the Blessed Virgin Mother of God. Modern editions of the *Fioretti* have dropped this section as a later addition of the 15th century, and so not authentic. But such an argument would have to drop all sayings of St. Francis as preserved in the *Fioretti*, because the entire work is a kind of "late" compilation. Far more reasonable is the position of the Martyr of Auschwitz, that like most of the sayings preserved in the *Fioretti*, this one has all the markings of something St. Francis said, even if not a word-for-word recording. Cf. Fehlner, "Una tesi. . .", cit., pp. 165-166.

glimpsed the stupendous mystery of the Immaculate Conception, like St. Francis, we can never surround the Virgin with too much praise, with praise objectively too grand for her, for the simple reason that we can never match the praise the Triune God has already showered on the first-born daughter and handmaid of the most High King and Father, Mother of His only-begotten Son, and spouse of the Holy Spirit.

But we must try both in word and in deed to imitate the *Salute* of St. Francis to the Virgin, which indeed expresses his response to the love of Mary for him and for all the redeemed of her Son, just as her crowning in heaven by the Blessed Trinity expresses the love of the Father for Mary so great that He entrusted His beloved Son to her and her womb only, the love of the Son so great that He yearned to be her Son as well as Son of the Father and so our brother, the love of the Holy Spirit so great that He desired above all as Creator Spirit to have Mary as His spouse and instrument in the greatest work of creation, the Incarnation and redemptive salvation of the human family (St. Maximilian, *SK* 1320).

In the light of this it becomes clear why the promotion of total consecration to the Immaculate becomes so crucial – and the massive disinterest, so far, to the spiritual warfare this involves on the part of most Catholics, bishops included, becomes so tragic. There can be no resolution of the crisis of faith affecting all mankind, and not merely Catholics, unless all particular programs, good in themselves, rest on this most basic means of renewal. For the crisis at its origin is fruit of the deceptions of the professional liar who is a murderer (cf. Jn 8, 44). [Infidelity to the truth is linked to that infidelity to Marian purity and is revealed in the massive pursuit of systematic murder of the innocent]. Without the Immaculate there can be no victory of wisdom in the academic order, of prudence in the political, of justice in the economic, of sanctity in the personal. But with her total victory is assured, for she has destroyed all heresy throughout the world. Just this concentrated synopsis of history was given when the Holy of Holies in heaven was opened to the vision of the beloved disciple entrusted to the Mother of God, that disciple saw revealed the Woman who is the Ark of the Covenant, the bearer of the victory and salvation which is her Firstborn, Jesus, to the rest of His brethren (cf. Rev. 11, 19 ff).

This is God's will, not arbitrary but supremely wise, an ordinance which is the key to understanding both the Incarnation and the rest of creation. It is clearly what stands behind the axiom of Scotus: *potuit, decuit, ergo fecit*. If we wish to understand, speculatively and practically, how the mysteries of faith are possible, we must seek to discover the primary *decuit* which stands behind them. Then we shall grasp why the *fecit* or what the charity of the Father has wrought is so grand: the Incarnation and Redemption. In a word, the clue is the Immaculate Conception, and that ultimately is what stands behind the title of chapter 8 of *Lumen Gentium* of Vatican II: "The Virgin Mary in the mystery of Christ and of the Church."

THE IMMACULATE CONCEPTION
AND THEOLOGICAL ANTHROPOLOGY

Mary Shivanandan, S.T.D.

> In these reflections. . . I wish to consider primarily that "pilgrimage of faith" in which the Blessed Virgin advanced, faithfully preserving her union with Christ.[1]

It may seem strange to choose this thought from Pope John Paul II's encyclical letter, *Redemptoris Mater* to introduce a discussion on the dogma of the Immaculate Conception. Surely the Immaculate Conception is about Mary's freedom from the carnal concupiscence of original sin. In the perspective of John Paul II's anthropology, however, it makes eminent sense. In order to present Paul VI's teaching of *Humanae Vitae* to a new post-modern generation, John Paul II saw the need to go beyond the moral precept to its anthropological foundation. In that context, faith assumes a pivotal place. It is not a question here of simple faith in the Magisterium per se but of an orientation of the whole human person. In other words, it is a question of the theological virtue of faith.

Faith has been at the center of John Paul II's academic and ecclesiastical concerns from the beginning. His doctoral

---

[1] John Paul II, *Mother of the Redeemer* (*Redemptoris Mater*) *Encyclical Letter, March 25, 1987* (Boston: St. Paul Books & Media, 1987), 4. Henceforward references to *Redemptoris Mater* will be cited in the text as *RM* and the section number. In *Mulieris Dignitatem:* Apostolic Letter "On the Dignity of Women (*Origins*, 18, 17 [Oct. 6, 1988]) John Paul II notes that the encyclical "develops and updates teaching contained in chapter 8 of the Dogmatic Constitution on the Church, *Lumen Gentium.*" Henceforward references to *Mulieris Dignitatem* will be cited in the text as *MD* and the section number. Similarly references to *Lumen Gentium* will be cited in the text as *LG* and the section number.

thesis at the Angelicum, *Faith According to St. John of the Cross,* explored the experience of faith in the writings of the Carmelite mystic. There he discovered that the soul truly adheres to theological truths. The actual union with the divine takes place in love. The mystic encounters God as a person and union takes place through the total surrender of the lover to the beloved.

While this was the beginning of John Paul II's analysis of faith in the life of the Christian, his own pilgrimage of faith has carried him to deeper insights, especially from his study of the person and love. From this he has come to see the spousal nature of faith and its essential role in love. St. Paul in 1 Corinthians 13 gives the magnificent definition of love and its primacy over all spiritual gifts. He ends with:

> At present we see dimly as in a faulty mirror, but then we shall see face to face. Now we know in part, but then I will know Him as He knows me. Now we have faith, hope and love, these three, but the greatest of these is love (1 Cor. 13: 12-13).

In some contemporary catecheses, this passage has been a pretext for devaluing the role of faith and separating it from love. It has often resulted in the dismissal of the Church's teaching role, especially in the area of sexual love. In reality, as John Paul II shows in *Redemptoris Mater*, the two cannot be separated. Mary's purity of faith is an essential aspect of her purity of heart and intrinsic to the grace of the Immaculate Conception.

In this paper I hope to show: (1) the nature of Mary's faith, (2) its relationship to the grace of the Immaculate Conception, (3) her faith and the grace of virginity, (4) the spousal nature of faith and the relationship to our own pilgrimage of faith. My sources will be primarily John Paul II's own writings, supplemented by contributions from other theologians and Scripture scholars.

John Paul II begins the encyclical by linking the blessing announced by the angel at the Annunciation with the blessing of Ephesians 1: 4-7 in which mankind has been chosen in Jesus Christ "*before the foundation of the world* that we should be holy and blameless before him" (*RM*, 7-8). This divine plan includes everyone, but refers especially to the woman, Mary, chosen to be the mother of the Redeemer. The address "full of grace" (*kecharitomene*) John Paul II links to the election of Ephesians. Grace in biblical language, he reminds us "means a special gift, which, according to the New Testament has its source in the Trinitarian life of God Himself, God who is love" (*RM*, 8). A "seed of holiness" springs from this gift and permeates those chosen. Mary, chosen as the Mother of the Son, is entrusted to the Spirit of holiness. From the first moment of her conception, Mary was preserved from the inheritance of original sin. She belonged to Christ, receiving life from Him to whom she gave earthly life in the Incarnation. This grace "determines the extraordinary greatness and beauty of her entire being" (*RM*, 11). As witness to God's destiny for us all to be sons in the Son, she remains a "sign of hope."

These opening paragraphs of the encyclical have placed Mary in the perspective of the entire plan of salvation. The grace of original innocence lost by our first parents has been restored to her through the merits of her Son. Yet she was destined to live like all mankind in a world estranged from God by the Fall. She journeyed like us on a "pilgrimage of faith." John Paul II turns in the encyclical to Mary's visit to her cousin Elizabeth to highlight the final words spoken by Elizabeth: "And blessed is she who believed that there would be a fulfillment of what was spoken to her from the Lord" (Lk. 1:45). He calls these words of *fundamental importance* and specifically links them to the title "full of grace." To quote John Paul II:

The *fullness of grace* announced by the angel means the gift of God himself. "*Mary's faith*, proclaimed by Elizabeth at the Visitation, indicates *how* the Virgin of Nazareth *responded to this gift* (*RM*, 12).

It is noteworthy in this passage that John Paul II identifies the gift as a Person, God Himself. In giving the "obedience of faith" Mary is entrusting herself to God with full submission of intellect and will. While Mary *believes* the words of the angel concerning her role in the eternal plan of salvation, with her *fiat* she commits herself, rather, abandons herself to the author of the plan, God Himself (cf. *RM*, 18).

This phrase, "blessed is she who believed," John Paul II considers a kind of 'answer key' to the truth of Mary. While "full of grace", she is present eternally in the mystery of Christ, it is through her faith that she became a sharer in the mystery (cf. *RM*, 19). Through all the vicissitudes of her life from Bethlehem to the Cross, Mary "is in contact with the truth about her Son only in faith and through faith" (*RM*, 17). Mary's fiat, therefore, is in stark contrast, as the Fathers of the Church have so often pointed out, to the doubt and disobedience of Adam and Eve. It is this disobedience and doubt of God's goodness and the world as gift that was the original sin. As John Paul II says in *The Theology of the Body: Human Love in the Divine Plan*,[2] Adam and Eve rejected the Father and opened themselves to what comes from the world. They questioned the gift. They could no longer receive each other as a disinterested gift, which is the true meaning of purity of heart or chastity. John Paul II contrasts Mary's words in the Magnificat with the 'suspicion' which the 'father of lies' sowed in the heart of the first woman, Eve. Mary, the New Eve, "boldly proclaims the *undimmed* truth about God: the holy and almighty God, who from the beginning is *the source of all gifts,* he who 'has done great things' in her as well as in the whole universe" (*RM*, 37).

---

[2] Boston, MA: Pauline Media and Books, 1997, 5/28/1980

According to Jean-Pierre Batut, professor of dogmatic theology at the Seminary of Paris, when it comes to the chastity of Jesus, "the Virgin alone truly understands her Son."[3] Because we are subject to carnal concupiscence from original sin, we can only begin to understand it through gradual conversion in Christ. In discussing the temptations of Christ, Aquinas makes a distinction between two kinds of temptation: those of the flesh and the world; and those, which have Satan as the direct author. It is important to understand the biblical meaning of flesh in this context as not the human body but the tendency, as a result of original sin, for man to direct his thoughts and desires towards earthly concerns and away from God. Even when Baptism has freed us from original sin, there remains in us a tendency towards evil – traditionally called concupiscence. While it only becomes sin when the will consents – and it can be overcome through effort and the grace of Christ – we are never in this life free from the tendency.[4]

When Adam and Eve were tempted in the Garden, they were both innocent, meaning their existence was oriented towards God. The temptation that comes directly from the tempter is not centered on desire for the goods of this world but attacks man's faith in God and His promises. That is why, according to Batut, the temptation in the third chapter of Genesis is "*absolutely the only one* to which we can. . . refer Christ's temptation."[5] Christ's very mode of existing as Son is to be wholly oriented towards God in loving obedience. In Matthew 4:3, the devil begins: "If you are the Son of God . . ." revealing that his aim is to destroy His Sonship. Original sin, then, begins the moment man *distrusts* God and accepts the tempter's *disfigurement* of God. By their choice, Adam and Eve separated themselves from God in order to cling to the things of this world. From this perspective, it was, like every sin, says

---

[3] Jean-Pierre Batut, "The Chastity of Jesus and the Refusal to Grasp," *Communio: International Catholic Review* 24 (Spring, 1997): 6.

[4] Ibid., 6-7

[5] Ibid.

Batut, "a sin against chastity – in its effects and its roots. For chastity . . . bears first of all on God."[6] Batut's analysis of Jesus' chastity helps us to understand better the reason John Paul II considers Elizabeth's praise of Mary's faith a key to her inmost reality and her purity of heart.

Purity of heart, according to Ysabel de Andia, "is primarily defined by the object of one's love, and there is only one object of love for the human heart, God."[7] The foundation of monotheism is the revelation of a unique God who "requires an exclusive love," in other words, it requires purity of heart.[8] "A pure heart," she notes, "is a heart whose whole love is God, a heart which loves all creatures, which loves itself, in God and for God."[9] John Macquarrie in an article on the Immaculate Conception describes original sin as essentially alienation from God, which brings about alienation from one's own true nature as well as other human beings. He equates grace with being in right relation with God. To be full of grace is the opposite condition of the state of original sin. With the Immaculate Conception, "alienation has been overcome, the channels from God are open, the moment is ripe for the Incarnation."[10] Macquarrie goes on to state that "Mary's righteousness is faithful obedience to God, summed up in the famous words, "Be it done unto me according to thy word" (Lk. 1:39)."[11]

Joseph Cardinal Ratzinger describes Mary as a "person who is totally open . . . and has placed herself . . .without fear

[6] Ibid., 10.
[7] Ysabel de Andia, "Purity of Heart," *Communio:Internationl Catholic Review* 16 (Spring, 1989): 37
[8] Ibid.
[9] Ibid., 38. The heart of Christ on the cross is the source of purity of heart, since it vanquished all impurity.
p. 49.
[10] John Macquarrie, "Immaculate Conception," *Communio: International Catholic Review* 7 (Summer, 1980): 109-110.
[11] Ibid., 111. Jacques Servais citing von Balthasar, notes that "sin brings about isolation and thwarts solidarity with others." See "Mary's Role in the Incarnation," *Communio: International Catholic Review* 30 (Spring, 2003): 21.

for her own destiny, in the hand of God."[12] She lives "so that she is a place for God."[13] He considers grace a *correlative idea*:

> It does not concern an attribute belonging to an individual self, but refers to a relationship between an I and a you, between God and a human being. Therefore we could translate "You are full of grace" as "You are full of the Holy Spirit. Your life is bound up with God."[14]

I.   The Grace of Virginity

Let us turn now to the biblical scholar, Ignace de la Potterie, and his exegesis and interpretation of Luke 1: 26-28, specifically the meaning of *Kecharitomene*, full of grace.

While accepting the Byzantine tradition in the East and the medieval in the West that this inspired biblical phrase indicates Mary's perfect holiness, he offers a further refinement. Noting that the verb (*charitoun*) used by Luke is only used elsewhere in the New Testament in Ephesians 1:6, which refers to mankind's eternal election, he shows that the form of the verb used denotes an action which is causative and effects something in the object. The very form *kecharitomene* in the perfect passive participle indicates that Mary has *already been transformed by grace*.[15] De la Potterie then cites the Fathers of the Church that the sanctification has taken place in view of Mary becoming the mother of the Son of God. It will take place virginally by the power of the Holy Spirit. The grace that has been given has inspired in Mary a desire for virginity. He cites St Bernard's interpretation that the grace operative in her was "the grace of her virginity."[16]

From this perspective, he sees the exegesis of this passage as helping to establish more firmly the dogma of the

---

[12] Joseph Ratzinger, "You are Full of Grace," *Communio: International Catholic Review* 16 (Spring, 1989): 58.

[13] Ibid., 60.

[14] Ibid., 59.

[15] Ignace de la Potterie, *Mary in the Mystery of the Covenant*, trans. Bertrand Buby, (Bombay: St. Pauls, 1995), 58-9.

[16] Ibid., 60.

Immaculate Conception. The biblical meaning of grace and the meaning given by the dogma coincide. Grace takes away sin. Mary, from the first moment of her conception, was preserved from all sin and all its consequences, especially concupiscence. It is equally important from an exegetical and theological point of view, according to de la Potterie, that this sanctification be a preamble for Mary's divine and virginal maternity. In this sense, exegesis can help to illuminate the dogma further.[17] The virginal birth is the indispensable "sign" for those who believe in Jesus "to discover in him the mystery of divine filiation."[18]

The verses speak of both a *virginitatis carnis* and a *virginitatis cordis.* Conception and birth are both physical, but it will be brought about by the Holy Spirit. The corporeal dimension mentioned in verses 28, 34, and 38 leads into the spiritual virginity of Mary. This is the virginity that is proposed to all believers. The fruit of spiritual virginity is total dedication to God and submission to His word. At this point, Ignace de la Potterie cites Romano Guardini as describing this attitude as fundamentally Marian. It is also spousal. The Daughter of Zion was also the spouse of Yahweh, the symbol of the covenant. "The *virginity* of Israel is nothing other, definitely, than the purity of her *spousal* relationship with God."[19] Mary's desire to live fully for God in virginity is, therefore, also the desire to live this spousal relationship with God. It is, in fact, Mary's desire to be everything to God that precedes the conception and virgin birth.[20] Just as in a human marriage, desire "precedes sex," so Mary's desire for God has a spousal character which is expressed by her virginity.[21]

---

[17] Ibid., 60-61.

[18] Ibid., 169.

[19] Ibid.,182-183.

[20] John Paul II cites particularly Sts. Augustine and Leo the Great among the Fathers of the Church who held that Mary conceived in her mind first. *RM*, 13.

[21] De la Potterie, *Mary in the Mystery of the Covenant,* 184. De la Potterie cites S. Nobécourt for this insight.

II.   Mary's Faith as Spousal

In commenting on Mary's *fiat* de la Potterie notes that Luke's use of the optative, *genoito*, without a subject, which is unique to this passage in the New Testament, expresses a joyous desire on Mary's part, not a resigned submission. It shows her desire to cooperate completely in the Lord's design. It echoes Exodus 19:8 where the People of God promise to do all that Yahweh commands at the time of the ratification of the Covenant of Mount Sinai. By her *fiat,* she becomes the personification of the Daughter of Zion.[22] Equally, John Paul II stresses the completeness of her submission. For example, he states: "She responded . . . *with all her human and feminine I,* and this response of faith included both perfect cooperation with 'the grace of God that precedes and assists' and perfect openness to the action of the Holy Spirit, who constantly brings faith to completion by his gifts" (*RM*, 13).

John Paul II points out that Mary's *fiat* was decisive on the human level. She uttered it in a faith equal to that of Abraham. Just as Abraham's faith initiated the Old Covenant so Mary's initiated the New. "Through this faith," John Paul II says, "Mary is perfectly united with Christ in his self-emptying" (*RM*, 13, 14).

When John Paul II refers to Mary's *"human and feminine I"* he is invoking all the richness of his reflections on the nature of the human person as masculine and feminine and their communion.[23] Particularly in his reflections on Genesis 1 – 4:1, he shows the meaning of the creation of man and woman in dual unity as similar yet different. They are similar in their humanity as persons with all that that encompasses, that is, self-knowledge, self-determination, and self-consciousness.[24] Each is in a unique relationship with God – "partner of the Absolute" as John Paul

---

[22] Ibid., 75, 182.

[23] Cf. John Paul II, *Mulieris Dignitatem*, "Mary's response reveals her personal and feminine I." With her *fiat*, Mary becomes the authentic subject of the Covenant, 4.

[24] For further discussion on the nature of the person – an "I" – and interpersonal communion, see *Mulieris Dignitatem,* 7.

II's expresses it. The only difference is that they are a different bodily manifestation of the person. Their bodies are nuptial, which means that in their sexual constitution they are designed for love. They are created as fundamentally open to each other and can only find themselves by a sincere mutual self-giving.[25]

In his commentary on Ephesians 5:21-33, which causes so much grief to contemporary feminists, John Paul II takes pains to stress the bi-subjectivity in St. Paul's head-body analogy. It applies both to Christ's union with the Church and human marriage. Only if each is truly a subject capable of giving him or herself can there be true communion. Yet there is a difference in the manner in which they give themselves to each other.[26] Although the union is reciprocal, it is the husband who initially loves and the wife who is loved. In the Apostolic Letter, *Mulieris Dignitatem*, the Pope says that the woman is entrusted to the man as a task, but she is also a subject responsible for herself (cf. *MD*, 14). Further on, he notes that the husband is commanded to love his wife as his own flesh. In this love, there is a fundamental affirmation of the woman as person (cf. *MD*, 24). In the order of love, "it is the bridegroom who loves and the bride who is loved" (*MD*, 29).

Again in the head-body analogy, John Paul II stresses that both men and women stand on the side of the Church collectively as bride in relation to Christ the bridegroom. "In this way," he writes, "being the bride, and thus the 'feminine' element, becomes a symbol of all that is human" (*MD*, 25). This is a theme that has been developed by women mystics such as Julian of Norwich and St. Brigid of Sweden.[27] Among contem-

---

[25]For John Paul II, two key passages of *Gaudium et Spes*, 22 and 24, hold the key to his anthropology. The first proclaims that only in the mystery of Christ does the mystery of man take on new light and the second, that in the manner of the Trinity only by becoming a sincere gift to another can man find himself. John Paul II applies *GS* 22, especially to the mother of Christ. "Only *in the mystery of Christ* is *her mystery made fully clear*" (*RM*, 4).

[26] John Paul II, *Theology of the Body*, 8/25/1982.

[27]See Prudence Allen, *The Concept of Woman: The Early Humanist Reformation 1250-1500.* (Grand Rapids, MI. 1985), 366-380, 398-428.

porary theologians, besides von Balthasar, it has been especially developed by David L. Schindler.[28]

Taking as his starting point Alexander Schmemann's *For
the Life of the World*,[29] Schindler "indicates the centrality of the
nuptial relation, or indeed the sacrament of matrimony, in
understanding the biblical God's relation in Christ to the world
– that is, in and through the Church."[30] Schindler also notes a
passage from Schmemann where he links the sacrament of
matrimony with the one who has always stood at the very heart
of the Church's life as the purest expression of human love and
response to God – Mary, the Mother of Jesus:

> In her love and obedience, in her faith and humility [Mary] accept-
> ed to be what from all eternity all creation was meant to be: the tem-
> ple of the Holy Spirit, the *humanity* of God. She accepted to give
> her body and blood – that is her whole life – to be the body and blood
> of the Son of God, to be *mother* in the fullest and deepest sense of
> this world, giving her life to the Other and fulfilling her life in Him.
> She accepted the only true nature of each creature and all creation:
> to place the meaning and, therefore, the fulfillment of her life in God
> . . . This response is total obedience in love; not obedience *and* love,
> but the wholeness of the one as the totality of the other.[31]

In other words, Mary's faith in response to God is spousal.
John Paul II also accents the spousal nature of Mary's fiat:

> It is significant that Mary, recognizing in the words of the divine
> messenger the will of the Most High and submitting to his power,

---

[28] In addition to David L. Schindler, James Heft notes the prominence of
the masculine-feminine polarity in von Balthasar's writings. "When he
[von Balthasar] speaks of Mary as the perfect contemplative, it is because
she is totally open to receiving the Word. In this she is totally feminine."
See "Marian Themes in the Writings of Hans Urs von Balthasar,"
Communio: International Catholic Review 7 (Summer, 1980): 131.

[29] Alexander Schmemann, *For the Life of the World* (Crestwood, NY: St.
Vladimir's Seminary Press, 1998 [1963])

[30] David L. Schindler, "Creation and Nuptiality: A Reflection on
Feminism in Light of Schmemann's Liturgical Theology," *Communio:
International Catholic Review* 28 (Summer, 2001): 270.

[31] Schmemann, *For the Life of the World*, 83-84, as quoted in Schindler,
"Creation and Nuptiality," 272.

says: "Behold, I am the handmaid of the Lord: let it be done to me according to your word (Lk. 1:38). It can be said that this *consent to motherhood* is above all *a result of her total self-giving to God in virginity.* Mary accepted her election as Mother of the Son of God, guided by spousal love, the love that totally consecrates a human being to God (*RM*, 39).

Her motherhood, continues John Paul II, is "completely pervaded by her spousal attitude as the handmaid of the Lord" (*RM*, 39). In *Mulieris Dignitatem*, John Paul II lays great stress on woman's spousal nature. It is linked to what he calls the order of love. "Only a person can love and only a person can be loved" (*MD*, 29).

Acknowledging this order of love is essential in order to understand the dignity and vocation of women. The fact that it is the woman who receives love in order to love in return cannot be confined just to the spousal nature of marriage. It reaches out to all her interpersonal relationships. By reason of her femininity, a woman, represents a particular value. In this sense, John Paul II speaks of a special kind of "prophetism" that belongs to women in their femininity. Michele Schumacher, in continuity with John Paul II's thought, notes the following:

> The dignity of woman is . . . biblically demonstrated within the order of love as a pure *grace*, as a completely unmerited gift, whereby she accomplishes her "prophetic" mission of manifesting the order of love and the truth that every human being is eternally loved in Christ. By the very fact that she *is loved*. . . she manifests the nature of the Church (as Bride) in relation to Christ (the divine bridegroom.[32]

From consciousness of being loved, the woman has an awareness that God has entrusted the human being to her in a special way and this constitutes her fundamental vocation (cf. *MD*, 30). It is intimately associated with both consecrated virginity and motherhood. As John Paul II notes:

[32] Michele Schumacher, "The Prophetic Vocation of Women and the Order of Love," *Logos* 2 (Spring, 1999): 155.

This "prophetic" character of women in their femininity finds its highest expression in the Virgin Mother of God. She emphasizes, in the fullest and most direct way, the intimate linking of the order of love – which enters the world of persons through a woman – with the Holy Spirit (*MD*, 29).

III. Mary's Motherhood and the Immaculate Conception

Mary's faith, united with love, is fruitful. Indeed only if faith and love are united can they be truly fruitful. United they lead to life, separated to death. Some of the great tragedies of drama and opera portray a great love outside the moral law. Not to mention the devastation caused by the trivialization of love in our culture and its separation from truth. Equally destructive is faith without love. It has spawned, and continues to spawn, religious wars. On the individual level it is Pharisaic. Ratzinger affirms that the Marian dimension of the Church "involves the heart, affectivity, and thus fixes faith solidly in the deepest roots of man's being."[33]

Motherhood is the ordinary fruitfulness of spousal love. In *The Theology of the Body: Human Love According to the Divine Plan*, John Paul II, commenting on Genesis 4:1, "I have gotten a man with the help of the Lord", says that "the mystery of femininity is manifested and revealed completely by means of motherhood."[34] He immediately relates it to Mary's motherhood:

> The Bible (and subsequently the liturgy), with its characteristic simplicity, honors and praises throughout the centuries "the womb that bore you and the breasts that you sucked." These words constitute a eulogy of motherhood, of the female body in its typical

---

[33]Joseph Ratzinger, "Thoughts on the Place of Marian Doctrine and Piety in Faith and Theology as a Whole," *Communio: International Catholic Review* 30 (Spring, 2003): 159. "Only the Marian dimension secures the place of affectivity in faith and thus ensures a fully human correspondence to the reality of the incarnate Logos." p. 153.

[34] *Theology of the Body,* 3/12/80.

expression of creative love. And they are the words referred in the Gospel to the Mother of Christ, the second Eve."[35]

In *Mulieris Dignitatem*, in which he addresses the dignity and vocation of women, John Paul II places motherhood, both physical and spiritual, within the context of the fundamental nature of woman. Motherhood implies from the beginning a special openness to the new person. In this openness, in conceiving and giving birth to a child, the woman discovers herself through a sincere gift of self (cf. *MD*, 18). Citing yet again Eve's exclamation in Genesis 4:1 "I have brought a man into the world with the help of the Lord", John Paul II notes that "motherhood is linked to the personal structure of the woman and to the personal dimension of the gift" (*MD*, 18).

In neither *Mulieris Dignitatem* nor *Redemptoris Mater* does John Paul II give much space to the biophysiological and psychological aspects of motherhood, although he gives due weight to what he calls the woman's greater contribution in the bearing and nurturing of the child. He is intent, rather, in highlighting Mary's spiritual motherhood. It is in the dimension of Mary's faith that he presents Mary's spiritual motherhood. Key to his thought are two passages in Luke's Gospel, namely Luke 1:32 where the woman cries out in blessing of Mary's physical motherhood, to which Jesus responds: "Blessed rather are those who hear the word of God and keep it;" and Jesus' response when told that His mother and brothers are waiting for Him: "My mother and brothers are those who hear the word of God and keep it." The Virgin Mary became His first disciple because she was the first to hear the word of God and keep it (cf. *RM*, 20). At the marriage feast of Cana, she presents herself as the *spokeswoman of her Son's will.* She appears at the wedding feast as *believing in Jesus.* It is her faith that evokes the sign, which stirs the disciple's faith.

---

[35] Ibid.

Ignace de la Potterie also stresses her spiritual motherhood. After an extensive treatment of the Christological meaning of the marriage feast of Cana, he brings out what he calls its "profound mariological meaning."[36] Among the many insights from a careful exegesis, he points out that the words of Mary to the servants, " Do whatever he tells you" are the final words of Mary preserved in the New Testament. As such they can be considered her spiritual testament. They are an invitation to listen to Jesus and do whatever He asks. This means that "she incites the disciples to docility and to obedience with regard to the word of Jesus, in other words, to believe in him."[37] Recent exegesis has shown that "do whatever he tells you," is taken from the Covenant formula. Thus she is the first to urge the "servants," namely the disciples, to perfect obedience and so become the new people of God.[38]

Mary's spiritual motherhood is definitively realized at the foot of the cross when Jesus presents her to John. Her new motherhood stems from the accomplishment of the Paschal Mystery. John Paul II again links faith and love: "This 'new motherhood of Mary,' generated by faith, is *the fruit of the 'new' love* which came to definitive maturity in her at the foot of the Cross, through sharing in the redemptive love of her Son" (*RM*, 23). Jesus' words signify that this new motherhood is linked to the Church, symbolized by the disciple John. John Paul II concludes that "in the redemptive economy of grace, brought about through the action of the Holy Spirit, there is a unique correspondence between the moment of the Incarnation of the Word and the moment of

---

[36] De la Potterie, *Mary in the Mystery of the Covenant*, 236. He relates it to the title Jesus gives her, "Woman" and the double role she plays in the episode as spouse and as mother. The title "Woman" appears again when Jesus addresses His mother on Calvary. "By this appellation, he places a certain distance between Himself and their former relationship, that of mother-son, but, at the same time, he opens up a new perspective: and he entices her into accepting another relationship with him in the mystery of salvation, beyond the maternal and familial" 240.

[37] Ibid., 240.

[38] Ibid., 240-241.

the birth of the Church" (*RM*, 24). The person who joins them is Mary. Through the "fullness of grace" proclaimed at the Annunciation, Christ prepared His mother to become "mother in the order of grace" for all people (cf. *RM*, 39). By linking her so strongly with the Church, Vatican Council II highlighted her role in the life of the Church. She is present with the Apostles at the time of Pentecost and continues to be present throughout the ages. As *Lumen Gentium* says, "*the mother of God is a figure of the Church* in the matter of faith, charity and perfect union with Christ" (*LG*, 63).

John Paul II stresses particularly her faith. Mary as Virgin believed she would conceive God's Son. As handmaid of the Lord she continued in *perfect fidelity* to the person and mission of her Son; believing and obeying, she became His mother. She is, therefore, present in the Church as a perfect model. By accepting God's word, the Church, virgin like Mary, also becomes a mother (cf. *LG*, 64). John Paul II sees in the Church's fidelity to Christ her spousal character (cf. *RM*, 44).[39] In Ephesians 5: 21-33, the model for the fidelity and total self-giving love of Christ and the Church is marriage. Nevertheless, John Paul II says it also has value for consecrated celibacy since the Church is also a Virgin. Such virginity, says John Paul II, "is the source of a special spiritual fruitfulness: *it is the source of motherhood in the Holy Spirit*" (*RM*, 44).

Mary's motherhood in the Church takes the form, according to John Paul II, particularly of directing her children towards Christ. She continues to say to each person: "Do whatever he tells you." "For every Christian, for every human being, Mary is the one who first "believed," and precisely with her faith as Spouse and Mother she wishes to act upon all those who entrust themselves to her as her children" (*RM*, 46). Might not one conclude that every Christian, both as consecrated celibate and married, is also called to a spousal and maternal role in the order of the Spirit? Only through

---

[39]This is also expressed in *Lumen Gentium* 64: "The Church herself is a virgin who keeps whole and pure the fidelity she has pledged to her spouse."

fidelity to God's word as expressed in the Church can the Christian be truly fruitful in imitation of Mary.

IV.   The Immaculate Conception and the People of God

Joseph Cardinal Ratzinger has succinctly outlined the tension in attitudes towards Mary leading up to Vatican Council II. Two diverse charismatic movements gained ascendancy in the period after World War I, Marian piety influenced by Marian apparitions, and the liturgical and biblical renewal. The motto of the latter was "through Christ to the Father" while the slogan of the Marian movement was "*per Mariam ad Jesum.*"[40] The two movements were almost equally represented at the Second Vatican Council. It is well known what happened in the vote on the document on the Church, *Lumen Gentium,* in October 1963; instead of a separate document on Mary, her treatise was included at the end of the document on the Church. Yet, in the aftermath of the Council, with the victory of the ecclesiotypical approach in Mariology, Mariology itself collapsed.

Pope Paul VI in *Marialis Cultus*[41] began to restore the balance. His stated aim in the Apostolic Exhortation was to examine in the light of the Council's teachings the relationship between Mary and the liturgy, and Mary as the model of the Church's living of the divine mysteries. He immediately highlights her faith. "Mary is the *attentive Virgin* who receives the word of God with faith" (*MC*, 17). Mary is not only a model for the Church in the exercise of divine worship, but she is also a teacher for the individual Christian (cf. *MC*, 21).

Devotion must keep in balance the place she occupies in the Church, as "the highest after Christ and the closest to us"

---

[40] Joseph Ratzinger, "Thoughts on the Place of Marian Doctrine and Piety in Faith and Theology as a Whole," *Communio: International Catholic Review* 30 (Spring, 2003): 148.

[41] Pope Paul VI "Devotion to the Blessed Virgin Mary: The Apostolic Exhortation *Marialis Cultus"* (February 2, 1974) in *The Pope Speaks* 19, 1 (1974): 49-87. Hereafter this will be cited in the text as *MC* and the section number.

(*MC*, 27). John Paul II echoes this dual character of Mary, also citing the Council; due to the fact that she is the Mother of God, "she far surpasses all other creatures" (*RM*, 10). She who has already reached the glory of the eschatological fulfillment of the Church still "cooperates with a maternal love" in the birth and development of the brothers and sisters of the Lord (cf. *RM*, 6).

Cardinal Ratzinger, quite rightly, points to another loss that occurred with the collapse of Mariology in the post-Vatican II period, namely, the loss of the feminine dimension of the Church.[42] The Fathers of the Church recognized that what was said of Mary also applies to the Church and vice versa. So the Church is also Virgin, Spouse, and Mother. In short, the *Ecclesia* is feminine and points to the domain of mystery beyond the sociological structure of the Church as the People of God. When the bridal love between Christ and the Church is ignored – the foundation upon which the whole of biblical and patristic talk about the Church actually hinges – the Church is only seen in a masculine structural way, eliminating all feminine dimensions, namely, virgin, bride, and mother. Yet, the body of Christ, the Church, is not primarily an organization but an *organism of Christ*. When the Church issues unpopular or challenging moral teachings such as *Humanae Vitae*, the response to an overly masculine Church structure is to chafe at the rules and see them as arbitrary impositions, not as the wise counsel of a loving mother.

The resurgence of the feminist movement in the late 1960s attracted new interest in Mary. Elizabeth Johnson represents one of the leading feminist voices writing on Mariological themes in post-Conciliar Mariology. Yet basic to her position is the notion that although the equal dignity of men and women is now understood by all, discrimination against women continues to be part of the theory and practice of the Church. Clearly Johnson only sees the Church as a masculine structure. While not totally rejecting Mary, she redefines her primarily as sister

---

[42] See Ratzinger, "Marian Doctrine," 152.

in her book on Mary, *Truly Our Sister*.[43]

It is significant that Mary's role as mother is down-played. It is not, it seems to me, primarily because being the Mother of God, *Theotokos,* and immaculately conceived, raises her above all women and causes her to be remote, but because motherhood itself is problematic in our contemporary culture. There is a providential aspect to the timing of the dogma of the Immaculate Conception in 1854. In the last half of the nineteenth century, contra-ception became endemic in industrial society.[44] In the one hundred and fifty years since the dogma was promulgated, we have seen the attack on motherhood increase exponentially. Not only has contraception become the norm, but conception is manipulated more and more by technological means.

In one of the apparitions to St. Bernadette at Lourdes, Mary identified herself as "The Immaculate Conception," not the one who was immaculately conceived. In essence as "The Immaculate Conception," she embodies all aspects of the grace announced by the angel, from the favor, to her response, to her motherhood of the Son of God. In this essay, following John Paul II, I have singled out Mary's response in faith. I would like to conclude by linking this aspect to acceptance of Paul VI's pivotal encyclical *Humanae Vitae.*

The massive rejection of *Humanae Vitae* began immediately after its promulgation in 1968 not only by the laity, but by priests and even bishops. A crisis in both morals and faith followed this rejection. While the two are intimately connected to purity of heart, faith takes priority. As Ysabel de Andia notes:

> Purity of heart is first of all godly before it is moral: it is the purity of faith. Here is the moment of the "true gnosis," in the sense

---

[43] Elizabeth Johnson, *Truly Our Sister: A Theology of Mary in the Communion of Saints* (New York: Continuum International Publishing Group, 2003).

[44] The vulcanization of rubber in 1843 made it possible for the first time to mass produce condoms.

meant by the Fathers of the Church. That is, it is the knowledge of the true God and of the true faith. St. Paul speaks of the "faith of the heart," (Rom. 10:10) and of the "circumcision of the heart" (Rom. 2: 28-29).[45]

Mary is the model of both dimensions of purity of heart. To hear the Word, it must be preached. Since 1968, there has been virtual silence from the pulpit on *Humanae Vitae*. At the same time, there has been an equally thunderous silence on Mary. Before Vatican Council II, there were numerous books of homilies on Mary. They ceased to be published after the Council. Yet, as Jacques Servais notes, following the example of St. Ignatius of Loyola: "Her prototypical act of faith draws [Mary] near to [believers] in their trials, in the night that must continually (and ever more deeply) endure until the culmination of the contemplation of the Passion and Cross."[46]

In conclusion, the 150th anniversary of the dogma of the Immaculate Conception provides a unique opportunity to re-present Mary as the one who goes before us in the pilgrimage of faith. She did not reject the married state so much as make a courageous choice to consecrate herself totally to the love of God. She was not simply a mother concerned about her Son but a "woman who helped to strengthen the apostolic community's faith in Christ. . . and whose maternal role was extended and became universal on Calvary" (*MC*, 37).

In the Immaculate Conception, Mary reveals to us the virginal, spousal, and maternal dimensions of the Church and of every disciple of Christ, whether consecrated to God in celibacy, marriage, or the single state. In her, faith and love are perfectly united. Restored to her proper role in the Church and in the hearts of Christians, she will help to heal its grievous divisions.

---

[45]Isabel de Andia, "Purity of Heart," 51.
[46] Servais, "Mary's Role," 6.

THE IMMACULATE CONCEPTION
IN THE THOUGHT OF ADRIENNE VON SPEYR

Fr. Donald H. Calloway, M.I.C.

Introduction

On December 8, 1955, Pope Pius XII made the following statement in an allocution to the Catholic Relief Services: "In honoring Mary, in every thought of her, We do homage to the superabundant mercy and love of the Redeemer of men, all of whom He wishes to draw into union with Himself through grace and His Holy Spirit."[1] Pius XII could not have chosen a better day than the Solemnity of The Immaculate Conception to mention the superabundant mercy and love of God; the Immaculate Conception is, indeed, the masterpiece of God's superabundant mercy and love. Yet, as we celebrate the 150th anniversary of that blessed day, December 8, 1854, when Blessed Pope Pius IX, overcome with such emotion that he burst into tears,[2] dogmatically declared that the Holy Mother of God had been conceived without original sin – thus declaring

[1] Pope Pius XII, "Allocution to Catholic Relief Services," December 8, 1955. *L'Osservatore Romano*, English Edition, December 12, 1955.
[2] The fact that Blessed Pope Pius IX burst into tears during the dogmatic pronouncement is attested to by the Most Reverend Dixon, Archbishop of Armagh, who was present at the ceremony: "His Holiness [Pius IX] who was ever remarkable for his devotion to the Holy Virgin, overpowered as if by the sense of the favor which God was conferring on him, in vouch-safing that he should be the instrument of rendering such an honor to this most beloved Mother, burst into tears. He went to read with a faltering voice, which betrayed the deepest emotion, the words 'declaramus' but for some minutes could proceed no further . . ." Cited by D.J. Kennedy, O.P. "The Dogma of the Immaculate Conception," *The Rosary Magazine*, December 1904:601.

her to be The Immaculate Conception (Apostolic Constitution *Ineffabilis Deus*) – we still have to ask ourselves whether or not we have taken full advantage of all the insights given to the Church over these last one hundred and fifty years concerning this unique mystery of God's superabundant mercy and love, The Immaculate Conception.

Historically, after the dogmatic declaration, the second half of the nineteenth century offered relatively few new insights into the mystery of the Immaculate Conception; even such original thinkers as Matthias Joseph Scheeben (1835-1888) and John Henry Cardinal Newman (1801-1890) had only minimal new theological insights. As a matter of fact, most of the studies on the Immaculate Conception being done at that time were of an historical nature, offering very little by way of new theological insights. While the fiftieth anniversary of the dogma of the Immaculate Conception in 1904 brought about a renewed interest in the topic – Pope St. Pius X even wrote an encyclical letter to commemorate the fiftieth anniversary of the dogma (*Ad Diem Illum Laetissimum*, February 2, 1904) – nevertheless, it would not be until the end of the second decade of the twentieth century that individuals in the Church would begin to advance new theological insights concerning this truth about Our Lady.

Undeniably, one of the most prominent and original thinkers on the Immaculate Conception during the early twentieth century was St. Maximilian Kolbe. His various writings on the Immaculate Conception were far ahead of his time and are, even today, considered to be some of the most provocative statements in Mariology.[3] As the century progressed on, it witnessed the promulgation of an encyclical by Pope Pius XII that initiated a Marian year to commemorate the centenary of the

[3]An overview of Kolbe's insights into the Immaculate Conception can be found in the following works: *Immaculate Conception and the Holy Spirit: The Marian Teachings of St. Maximilian Kolbe*. Fr. H.M. Manteau-Bonamy, O.P. Trans. Br. Richard Arnandez, F.S.C. (Libertyville: Franciscan Marytown Press, 1977); *The Kolbe Reader*. ed. Fr. Anselm W. Romb, O.F.M. (Libertyville: Franciscan Marytown Press, 1987).

dogma of the Immaculate Conception (*Fulgens Corona*, September 8, 1953). Once again this action by a supreme pontiff, similar to that of St. Pius X in 1904, served as a catalyst for renewed interest in Our Lady's Immaculate Conception; this is historically evidenced by the in-depth theological studies on the Immaculate Conception undertaken by the International Marian Academy in Rome from October 24 – November 1, 1954. The lasting fruit of this Congress was a ten-volume work by some of the most prominent scholars of the day.[4] It is truly an essential and invaluable resource for anyone interested in studying the Immaculate Conception.[5] Furthermore, shortly after this monumental event, such erudite figures as Fr. Marie-Dominique Philippe, O.P.[6], Fr. Urban Mullaney, O.P.[7], Fr. Juniper Carol, O.F.M.[8], and Fr. Hans Urs von Balthasar[9] offered stunning theological insights into this mystery.

In our own day, Pope John Paul II, a great Marian Pope, has expressed a desire for there to be renewed efforts in studies done on the mystery of the Immaculate Conception,

---

[4]*Virgo Immaculata: Acta Congressus Mariologici-Mariani Romae. Vol.1-10.* Academia Mariana Internationalis, 1958.

[5]Worthy of note is the fact that certain Mariological societies, besides participating in the International Marian Congress of 1954, also had national symposia on the theme of the Immaculate Conception, e.g., the Flemish Mariological Society, Spanish Mariological Society (Spain), Canadian Mariological Society, and the Mariological Society of America.

[6]Marie-Dominique Philippe, O.P. *Mary, Mystery of Mercy*. (Stockbridge, MA: Marian Press, 2002), originally published as three separate works, *Trois Mysteres de Misericorde* from 1958-1960.

[7]Urban Mullany, O.P., "The Immaculate Conception in God's Plan of Creation and Salvation," in *The Dogma of the Immaculate Conception: History and Significance*, ed. Edward D. O'Connor, C.S.C. (Notre Dame: University of Notre Dame Press, 1958).

[8]Juniper B. Carol, O.F.M. *A History of the Controversy Over the "Debitum Peccati."* Theology Series No.9 (St. Bonaventure, NY: Franciscan Institute Publications, 1978).

[9]Hans Urs von Balthasar, *Theo-Drama: Vol.III. Dramatis Personae, Persons in Christ*. Trans. Graham Harrison. (San Fancisco: Ignatius Press, 1992), originally published as *Theodramatik: Zweiter Band: Die Personem des Spiels, Teil 2: Die Personem in Christus* in 1978.

explicitly with the intention of "investigating new sources . . . to draw from them further starting points for theological research."[10] Regarding this desire, the Pope notes:

> A suitable opportunity to intensify this commitment [to Marian studies] will be the 150th anniversary of the definition of the dogma of the Immaculate Conception of Mary. The two Pontifical Marian Academies, each in its own sphere of activity and with its own competence, are called to make their contribution so that the observance may be an opportunity to renew the theological, cultural and spiritual endeavor to communicate to the men and women of our time the meaning and the genuine message of this truth of faith [The Immaculate Conception].[11]

Therefore, while recognizing that this symposium is not an official branch of either of the two Pontifical Marian Academies,[12] yet ardently desiring to respond to the call of the Holy Father that there be investigations into "new sources" for Marian research, the following paper seeks to present the Immaculate Conception in the thought of one of the most understudied mystics and Marian figures of the twentieth century, Adrienne von Speyr.

I.   Adrienne von Speyr: Life and Charism

In 1968, one year after the death of Adrienne von Speyr, Hans Urs von Balthasar noted that even though Adrienne had

---

[10]Pope John Paul II, "Mariological reflection with interdisciplinary contribution," Seventh Session of Pontifical Academies: October 29, 2002. *L'Osservatore Romano.* English Edition, November 13, 2002.

[11]Ibid.

[12]It should be noted that the Pope's desire has been very well received. For example, the Pontifical Theological Faculty 'Marianum' offered "The Dogma of the Immaculate Conception: Current Problems and Attempts at a Renewed Understanding," Fourteenth International Mariological Symposium, Rome, October 7-10, 2003; The International Pontifical Marian Academy offered "The Immaculate Conception: The Contribution of the Franciscans," Assisi, December 4-8, 2003. Also worthy of note is the Mariological Society of America's annual meeting to be held in Houston, Texas from May 19-22, 2004. The theme is "The Immaculate Conception: Calling and Destiny."

dictated well over sixty volumes of work and successfully published thirty-seven books, no one up to that point had taken "serious notice of her writings. No newspaper except Lucerne's *Vaterland* deemed her worthy of even a brief obituary notice."[13] Sadly, though thirty-six years have gone by, the situation has only slightly improved.[14] This seems almost impossible to believe in light of her gargantuan spiritual and theological achievements, profound mystical experiences, partnership in co-founding a secular institute, and overall influence on one of the greatest theologians of the twentieth century, Hans Urs von Balthasar. To this day, her insights into various theological fields remain relatively unknown among theologians, scholars and laity alike.[15] Thus, who is this mysterious figure that the modern world seems to have forgotten?

Adrienne was born in Switzerland on September 20, 1902, to Theodor and Laure von Speyr. Born into a Protestant (thought not very devout) family, her father was of German-Swiss descent and was an opthamologist; Adrienne's mother,

---

[13]Hans Urs von Balthasar, *First Glance at Adrienne von Speyr*. Trans. Antje Lawry & Sr. Sergia Englund, O.C.D. (San Francisco: Ignatius Press, 1981), 12.

[14]See, for example, Barbara Albrecht, *Eine Theologie des Katholischen. Einführung in das Werk Adrienne von Speyrs* (Einsiedeln: Johannes Verlag); vol.1: *Durchblick in Texten* (1972); vol.2: *Darstellung* (1973); Pierangelo Sequeri, "La mistica oggettiva di Adrienne von Speyr. Elaborazione dell'oggettività teologica di un carisma ecclesiale," *Revista di teologia di Lugano* 6 (2001): 91-104; Jacques Servais, "Per una valutazione dell'influsso di Adrienne von Speyr su Hans Urs von Balthasar," *Revista di teologia di Lugano* 6 (2001): 67-90. Also, Johann G. Roten, S.M. gave a presentation at the 2003 Catholic Theological Society of America Annual Convention, Cincinnati, June 5-8, titled "Adrienne von Speyr as Theologian." A synopsis of this presentation can be found in *CTSA Proceedings* 58 (2003): 124-125.

[15]In light of the heterodox theological tendencies that permeated western (English speaking) theological faculties in the post Vatican II Church, Regis Martin, writing in 1985, poignantly noted: "How very different the landscape of the Church might be today if, 20 years ago, publishers in this country [United States] had made available to us the works of von Speyr . . ." See Regis Martin, "Von Speyr's life of grace," *National Catholic Register*. December 29, 1985.

Laure, was of French-Swiss descent and was a housewife. Adrienne was the second child, having an older sister, Helen, and two younger brothers, Wilhelm and Theodor. The family was of good standing in the community and had a long history of well-respected occupations: bell makers, physicians, clergyman (Protestant), and businessmen.

As a young girl Adrienne exhibited an uncanny and perspicacious ability for learning; for example, she could read and write before she formally entered school. Her youth was like any other girls' youth – playing with dolls, visiting grandparents, and taking time for tea parties. Yet, she never quite got along with her mother. Her mother was harsh, cruel and cold. Most of what she learned about religion came from her grandmother and from occasional Sunday school classes she attended. Interestingly, she always seemed dissatisfied with the doctrine of Protestantism, even expressing to a local minister the opinion that clergymen should be celibate; she even found the public-style of confession practiced by the Salvation Army quite distasteful and in need of being done privately, that is, one-on-one. Remarkably, despite that fact that her environment was often times quite anti-Catholic, she seems to have been predisposed by grace for a truly Catholic understanding of Christianity. As a matter of fact, when she was six years old she had an encounter with a mysterious man that later in life she would identify as St. Ignatius of Loyola;[16] and at the age of nine, she gave a type of "lecture" to her fellow classmates concerning the Jesuits and their notion of *reservatio mentalis*.[17]

All throughout her youth and adult life Adrienne suffered from various types of physical difficulties: spondylitis, appendicitis, diabetes, tuberculosis in both lungs, arthritis, partial blindness, a heart attack and cancer. Yet, perhaps the "wound" that was the most intriguing was the one that she received when she was fifteen years old. In November of 1917 – while still a Protestant – she allegedly had a vision of

---

[16]See Adrienne von Speyr, *My Early Years*. Trans. Mary E. Hamilton & Dennis D. Martin (San Francisco: Ignatius Press, 1995), 32-33.
[17]Ibid., 41-42.

the Blessed Virgin Mary, surrounded by angels.[18] This experience left her with a mystical wound under her left breast for the rest of her life, the meaning of which would only become apparent when she met Hans Urs von Balthasar. This Marian experience would truly prove to be the beginning of a wonderful intimacy with the Virgin Mary that Adrienne would only fully come to know once she became Catholic. For the time being, she experienced a type of "faraway tenderness for the Holy Virgin."[19]

Due to her aptitude for learning, Adrienne decided to pursue medical school. Though her family was quite opposed to this decision – female doctors were practically unheard of in Switzerland in those days – she eventually achieved her goal and became one of the first female doctors in all of Switzerland. In 1927, she met the widower Emil Dürr, a history professor at the University of Basel. Emil and Adrienne were soon married and living a happy life in their respective careers; Adrienne also became the stepmother of Emil's two young boys. Unfortunately, Adrienne soon found herself a widow when in 1934 Emil died in an accident. She was left to care for the two boys, continuing in her occupation as a doctor.

In 1936, Adrienne married Werner Kaegi, the assistant of her late husband Emil. This was a happy marriage; however, as a result of her first husband's death, she struggled with the ability to fully pray the Our Father, especially the words 'Thy will be done'. Over the years she had made numerous efforts to try and speak to a Catholic priest, but none of these attempts were ever successful. It was at this point – shortly after having suffered a heart attack in 1940 – that she met one of the most learned men of the twentieth century, Fr. Hans Urs von Balthasar.

At the time of their meeting in the fall of 1940, von Balthasar was a Jesuit priest serving as the student chaplain

---

[18]Ibid., 166-167.
[19]Ibid., 167.

at the University of Basel. This encounter would serve as the beginning of a friendship that would last twenty-seven years and prove to be, as the learned Marianist Fr. Johann Roten phrased it: "a psychological and theological symbiosis."[20] After her death, von Balthasar himself adamantly insisted that her work was more important than his,[21] stating that after their meeting in 1940 their work "can never be neatly separated"[22] due to the fact that their common work comprises "two halves of a single whole, which has as its center a unique foundation."[23] Thus, after 1940, it is truly pointless to try and disentangle their work.[24] Yet, even in the light of such clear and unambiguous statements from von Balthasar, there are some renowned scholars that still continue to be perplexed over Adrienne's necessary place in von Balthasar's theological project.[25] Some miss the point altogether.[26]

As divine providence would have it, it was shortly after her meeting with von Balthasar that Adrienne became a Catholic on the feast of All Saints, November 1, 1940. After her conversion, she continued to work as a doctor, seeing some sixty to eighty patients a day.[27] It was not long after her conversion, however, that she began to experience ecstatic flights, stigmatization, bilocation, vicarious suffering, and

---

[20]Johann G. Roten, S.M., "The two halves of the moon: Marian anthropological dimensions in the common mission of Adrienne von Speyr and Hans Urs von Balthasar," *Communio: International Catholic Review* 16 (Fall, 1989): 421.

[21]See von Balthasar, *First Glance*, 13.

[22]von Balthasar, *Our Task*, 95.

[23]Hans Urs von Balthasar, *My Work: In Retrospect.* Trans. Fr. Brian McNeil, C.R.V. (San Francisco: Ignatius Press, 1993), 89.

[24]See von Balthasar, *Our Task*, 73.

[25]See, for example, Edward T. Oakes, *Pattern of Redemption: The Theology of Hans Urs von Balthasar* (New York: Continuum, 1994), esp. pp.3-4, 10-11, 300-305; Fergus Kerr, O.P., "Adrienne von Speyr and Hans Urs von Balthasar," *New Blackfriars* 79 (January 1998): 26-32.

[26]See Tina Beattie, "A Man and Three Women. Hans, Adrienne, Mary and Luce," *New Blackfriars* 79 (February 1998): 97-105.

[27]It is even noted that in her practice as a medical doctor she helped thousands of women from having abortions. See von Balthasar, *First Glance*, 32.

the Passion of the Lord during Holy Week. She began to go into ecstatic states where she would dictate[28] voluminously about such things as the Trinity, the Virgin Mary, the Communion of Saints, and a plethora of other theological topics. Perhaps the most impressive of her dictations were those that are considered commentaries and/or meditations on sacred Scripture. These biblical commentaries are simply stunning in their insights into the mystery of God's Word. Von Balthasar, for his part, played a very important role in all of these happenings.

After leaving the Jesuits – he left of his own free will, yet under the guidance of von Speyr – von Balthasar lived in the Kaegi household in order to do his theological writings and be available for the dictations. Together they founded a secular institute, the Community of St. John (*Johannesgemeinschaft*), which was dedicated to living a consecrated way of life while living in the world. Their common mission and spirituality would truly be monumental and unlike anything of its kind in twentieth century thought.[29] As it turns out, the wound Adrienne received in the vision of the Virgin Mary in 1917 served as a source of vicarious suffering and spiritual fruitfulness in her common task and mission with von Balthasar.

Adrienne suffered heroically during the last years of her life. She began to go blind around 1965, and was only able to sleep for two or three hours a night due to nocturnal ecstatic flights. On September 17, 1967, at the age of sixty-four, Adrienne died. Her final words were addressed to von Balthasar, her longtime friend and spiritual director. She simply stated: "Thank you, thank you, thank you."[30]

---

[28]It is important to note that most of the literary works attributed to Adrienne were not actually written by her hand but, rather, dictated to von Balthasar while she was in ecstasy; von Balthasar later edited and published them.

[29]Jacques Servais, "The *ressourcement* of contemporary spirituality under the guidance of Adrienne von Speyr and Hans Urs von Balthasar," *Communio: International Catholic Review* 23 (Summer, 1996): 300-321.

[30]von Balthasar, *Our Task*, 89.

Undeniably, Adrienne's ecclesial charism and mission have not been fully appreciated and understood. She remains a woman wrapped in mystery. Many do not desire to take her work seriously on a theological level because of the 'private revelation' dimension of her life and work.[31] This is most unfortunate; anyone who reads her work cannot help but be inspirited by her theological insights and orthodoxy.[32] Regardless of the fact that she was a woman who experienced all kinds of 'private revelations' and mystical experiences, if her orthodoxy were in question would Pope John Paul II in 1983 have requested that an International Colloquium take place to study her thought?[33] The Holy Father, in an audience with the one hundred and fifty participants of this colloquium, gave them his blessing in the following words: "With all my heart I invoke abundant divine graces for the organizers of this Colloquium and upon all of its participants."[34]

II.   Adrienne's Marian Thought

In light of all the above, it only seems natural that when dealing with such a profound mystic as Adrienne von Speyr that the Blessed Virgin Mary occupy a central, necessary place in her overall thought and spirituality; for it is impossible to be an authentic Christian mystic without having a Marian modality in

[31]See von Balthasar's insightful comments on this topic in von Balthasar, *First Glance*, 57-58.

[32]There are some, however, who do question her theological orthodoxy. For an interesting exchange on this debate see Anne Barbeau Gardiner (with Fr. Jacques Servais' response), "Correcting the Deposit of Faith? The Dubious Adrienne von Speyr," *New Oxford Review* (September 2002): 31-45.

[33]This colloquium took place in Rome in the fall of 1985. In anticipation of this event von Balthasar, in 1984, published the book titled *Our Task: A Report and a Plan*. The various presentations from this colloquium are contained in *La Missione Ecclesiale di Adrienne von Speyr: Atti del II Colloquio Internazionale del pensiero cristiano*, ed. Hans Urs von Balthasar. (Milan: Jaca Book, 1986).

[34]John Paul II, "To Seminar on Adrienne von Speyr," September 28, 1985. *L'Osservatore Romano*, English Edition, October 28, 1985.

one's relationship with the Trinity. The fact that Mary is at the core of Adrienne's thought is clearly evidenced when one reads her works;[35] there is hardly a work in which the Blessed Virgin Mary is not mentioned, and most of these contain substantial treatments of various themes dealing with the Holy Virgin. Yet, as is the case with most of Adrienne's work, her profound Mariological thought has gone relatively unnoticed – the exception being the theological project of Hans Urs von Balthasar.[36]

It is worth noting that the only book Adrienne completely planned and saw to completion on her own was a book on Mary: *Handmaid of the Lord*.[37] This work was written in 1946 and published in 1948 as *Magd des Herrn*. Von Balthasar, besides being her spiritual director and noting that she possessed an "almost incomprehensible familiarity with the Mother of the Lord"[38] also noted that when seeking to do a systematic reading of Adrienne's works the book, *Handmaid of the Lord*, should be read first.[39] This is due to the fact that Mary's *fiat* is at the core of Adrienne's spirituality and thought; any attempt at trying to understand Adrienne outside of a Marian modality will, in the end, prove to be a fruitless endeavor.[40]

[35]See the following excellent studies by Fr. Johann G. Roten, S.M. on the theme of Mary in the writings of Adrienne von Speyr: "Maria Und Die Theologische Biographie Adrienne Von Speyrs. Ein Versuch Narrativer Spiritualitat," *Ephemerides Mariologicae* 52 (2002): 267-293; "The two halves of the moon: Marian anthropological dimensions in the common mission of Adrienne von Speyr and Hans Urs von Balthasar," *Communio: International Catholic Review* 16 (Fall, 1989): 419-445.

[36]It can be surmised that in light of the fact that Pope John Paul II relies heavily upon the Mariological thought of Hans Urs von Balthasar that he is – at least implicitly – also relying (necessarily) upon the Mariological thought of Adrienne von Speyr. See, e.g., footnote #55 of the Apostolic Letter *Mulieris Dignitatem* where John Paul II explicitly mentions Hans Urs von Balthasar.

[37]Adrienne von Speyr, *Handmaid of the Lord*. Trans. E.A. Nelson (San Francisco: Ignatius Press, 1985).

[38]von Balthasar, *Our Task*, 70.

[39]See von Balthasar, *First Glance*, 248.

[40]The late John Cardinal O'Connor even claimed that Adrienne's *Handmaid of the Lord* is "Catholic theology at its most insightful and ele-

The fact that Adrienne underscores Mary's fundamental stance in relation to God as *handmaid* – though this in no way implies that she intended this relation to serve as a fundamental Mariological principle – serves to underscore her understanding that all of Mary's various relations to God (mother, bride, daughter, etc…), and all of her prerogatives and privileges (Immaculate Conception, Divine Motherhood, Perpetual Virginity, Assumption, Co-Redemptrix, Mediatrix, Queenship, etc …), manifest the reality that Mary, as she herself states in the Magnificat (Lk.1:38), is and does all things as *ancilla Domini*. It is this notion, Mary as handmaid, which serves as the starting point of Adrienne's theological project; this does not, however, rule out or exclude other fundamental approaches in the Marian thought of Adrienne; for example, Adrienne always presents Mary, whether in person or in mission, as a nuptial person – in this sense Mary is always the *nuptial handmaid*.

Thus, mindful that we are dealing with one of the most profound and understudied "Marian" mystics of the twentieth century, it only seems appropriate as we celebrate the 150th anniversary of the dogma of the Immaculate Conception to present and expose Adrienne's thought on this singular privilege of Our Lady. In doing this, however, it must be remembered that Adrienne was not a systematic thinker in Marian studies; her thoughts on this topic are not, therefore, collected in one systematic essay or book. Neither are her various statements to be interpreted against a strictly scientific theological backdrop; Adrienne was not an academic theologian, and her works should not be read as though she were. On the contrary, because she was a mystic, her expressions flow from the heart and were never intended to be placed in the same category as, for example, a strictly academic work in Mariology; this must be kept in mind throughout the duration of this paper. Nevertheless, this paper seeks to present her thoughts on this

gant." See John Cardinal O'Connor, "Pastoral Reflections on the Holy Sacrifice of the Mass. VIII: Mary, the Mother of Christ's Mass," *Catholic New York*, December 24, 1998.

topic by employing a thematic approach that can be gleaned from her various writings on the Virgin Mary. From these writings, I believe there are three specific areas where Adrienne has something to say concerning the Immaculate Conception: 1) Trinitarian Dimensions, 2) Mission, 3) Co-Redemptrix.

1) The Immaculate Conception: Trinitarian Dimensions

The Trinity is at the heart of all of Adrienne's theological expositions. Whether she is commenting on the mission of the prophets, confession, the mystery of death, or some other theological topic, there is always a Trinitarian dimension involved. This also proves to be the case with the mystery of the Immaculate Conception.

a) The Father & The Immaculate Conception

In most of the writings on the Immaculate Conception in past centuries it was often the case that the only Persons of the Trinity mentioned in conjunction with this great mystery were the Son and the Holy Spirit. Adrienne, on the other hand, emphatically holds the Immaculate Conception to be a "matter of the triune God."[41] Of course, past centuries would not have denied this dimension;[42] yet, it cannot be denied that God the Father seems to have been somewhat neglected in many theologians' treatment of this subject. Most likely this "neglect" was due to the theologians' desire to focus on the redemption wrought by the Son, and the sanctification achieved by the Holy Spirit – attempting to understand the sinlessness of Mary while trying to safeguard the divine prerogatives – without doing theological harm to either. It is easy to see, therefore, how the Father could be overlooked.

[41]Adrienne von Speyr, *Mary in the Redemption.* Trans. Helena M. Tomko. (San Francisco: Ignatius Press, 2003), 75.

[42]For example, St. Alphonsus de Liguori, in his acclaimed work *The Glories of Mary* has a section titled: "How fitting it was that each of the Three Divine Persons should preserve Mary from Original Sin." See *The Glories of Mary* (Brooklyn: Redemptorist Fathers, 1931), pp.287-317.

One century after the dogmatic definition, the integrity of the missions of the Son and the Holy Spirit having been safe-guarded, Adrienne has put the Father at the forefront of the mystery.

Adrienne gets to the heart of the Father's relation to the Immaculate Conception when she states that "in order to facilitate the Son's work, the Father redeems the Mother of God in advance, so that she might be capable of giving birth to the infant Redeemer."[43] This reveals that even though redemption is achieved by the Son, there also exists a redeeming role for the Father; the Father is not left out of the role of either redemption or sanctification. On the contrary, it is the Father who is the origin of both, though each person of the Trinity participates in a way proper to His person. To clar-ify this, Adrienne will state the following:

> The Father *gives* the redemption of the world to the Son, and the Son *accomplishes* it. Both are one in their will to redeem, but not in a simple identity of will, insofar as the Son has a human will and suffers. It is therefore possible to make something of a dis-tinction.[44]

Adrienne will affirm – as do all orthodox Christians – that "Mary is planned and created both from and for the Cross."[45] There would be no Immaculate Conception without the Cross of Jesus Christ. Yet, due to the fact that the work of redemption originates in the Father, she will also state that "the hour of the Cross is the hour of the Father."[46] What this means is that the Father is not unprepared for the reality that will happen to His eternal Son on the Cross. On the contrary, because of His fatherly providence in sending His Son to accomplish the redemption of the world, the Father makes preparations for the Son, even offering to the Son, as gift, the

---

[43] Adrienne von Speyr, *The Countenance of the Father*. Trans. David Kipp. (San Francisco: Ignatius Press, 1997), 128-129.
[44] von Speyr, *Mary in the Redemption*, 85.
[45] Ibid., 18.
[46] von Speyr, *The Countenance of the Father*, 71.

perfect fruit of His (the Son's) redemption, namely, the Immaculate Conception. Adrienne describes this action of the Father in the following way:

> Mary's Immaculate Conception can be called a gift of the Father to the Son. Nonetheless, Mary is redeemed naturally, that is to say, she is redeemed through the Son. But within this resides something similar to the Father accompanying the Son's work; a proof before the proof; an assurance, given to the Son en route by the Father, that everything will go according to plan.[47]

That the Father gives the Immaculate Conception as a gift to the Son as a fruit of His (the Son's) redemption, and as a cooperator in the Son's work of redemption, should come as no surprise to those conversant with sacred Scripture. In the Farewell Discourse of Jesus we are told that the Father has given to His Son, as gift, those that are to be redeemed and, as a consequence of that redemption, those who are to participate in the Son's redemptive mission (Jn.17:18, 24).[48] Therefore, if the disciples are gifts from the Father to the Son, how much more the woman who was to bear Him and cooperate with Him in the salvation of the world! She would of necessity, as a pre-redeemed gift from the Father, have to be immaculately conceived in order to fulfill her maternal role of giving flesh to the Second Person of the Trinity. Concerning this, Adrienne makes the following observation:

> With the mystery of her Immaculate Conception, Mary therefore stands at a point of intersection in the Trinity, because she is a gift both from the Son to the Father and from the Father to the Son; the Father is preeminent in this since it is he who gives her to the Son in order to be able to get his work underway in the first place.[49]

One last point that needs to be mentioned concerning Adrienne's presentation of the role of the Father in the

[47]von Speyr, *Mary in the Redemption*, 85.
[48]Jesus will also state that "no one can come to me unless the Father who sent me draws him." Jn. 6:44, 65.
[49]von Speyr, *Mary in the Redemption*, 18.

Immaculate Conception, and this should come as no surprise, is the presentation of the Immaculate Conception in nuptial (spousal) categories:

> In her Immaculate Conception, Mary has the distinctive characteristic of heralding the coming of the even greater purity of the Son and his divinity. She is like a wedding ring that the Father gives to the Son as a deposit to show that the work of redemption will succeed. The Father's gift [the Immaculate Conception] gushes forth through the Cross, but does so like a special rivulet that flows from the Father into the Mother.[50]

In this understanding, Adrienne presents the Father as giving the Immaculate Conception to the Son for the purpose of both divine motherhood and spiritual betrothal. In the spiritual betrothal sense, the Immaculate Conception stands as both archetype and mediatrix of the spousal union that occurs between God and man. Mary, as the Immaculate Spouse of Christ, is ultimately what the Father desires all human persons to be transformed into as the result of His Son's mission to die for the life of the world. The Immaculate Conception is simply the Father's pre-redemption gift to the Son.[51] Ultimately, it is the Father who prepares and gives the bride to His Son. Once again, these themes are very consonant with the sacred scriptures. One has only to think of the various Patriarchs and how each of them prepared a bride for his son, for example, Abraham – Isaac/Rebekah, Isaac – Jacob/Rachel.[52]

b) The Son & The Immaculate Conception

Concerning the relation that exists between the Second Person of the Trinity and the Immaculate Conception,

---

[50]Ibid., 85.

[51]In this sense, Mary's Immaculate Conception can be understood from a protological perspective. We, however, will acquire this 'immaculateness' from an eschatological perspective.

[52]It is also interesting to note how Jesus often refers to Mary as *woman*, a term in the Greek that can mean *bride*.

Adrienne certainly adheres to the orthodox, and dogmatically defined, teaching that Mary was preserved from original sin "in view of the merits of Christ."[53] While this definition has become common theological knowledge, Adrienne, while holding fast to it, nonetheless, builds her understanding of the relationship existing between the Son and the Immaculate Conception upon the preeminence of the Father and His relation to the Immaculate Conception. For example, Adrienne will state: "It cannot simply be said that the Son suffers on the Cross for the Mother. She is redeemed in a pre-light of the Cross. This demonstrates the magnanimity of the Father, a gift in advance from the Father to the Son."[54] In this sense the Father already knows, and has planned into the Son's work of redemption, the perfect fruit of His Son's sacrifice: the Immaculate Conception; and, yet, in some mysterious way, the Son really redeems Mary by His sacrifice on the Cross. Thus, in typical paradoxical form, Adrienne will state: "She [Mary] is the Immaculate on the grounds of the Son's pre-merit, which the Father recognizes and considers as something that has already been accomplished."[55]

Perhaps the above statements will make more sense when seen in the light of a specific event in the life of Christ recounted for us in the Gospel of John. At one point John the Baptist cries out, in response to the questions of some of his own disciples and fellow Jews, concerning the identity of the Christ: "He who has the bride is the bridegroom" (Jn.3:29a). What are we to make of this? We can offer a sound theological answer when we take into consideration Adrienne's thought on the Immaculate Conception; namely, the Father has prepared a bride for His Son, and already given her to His Son so that that same Son might always have before Him the perfect fruit of His forthcoming sacrifice. Furthermore, the gift that the Father has given to the Son is the Immaculata, the bridal-mother. In other

---

[53]Blessed Pope Pius IX, *Ineffabilis Deus*, December 8, 1854. (Boston: Daughters of St. Paul), 21.
[54]von Speyr, *Mary in the Redemption*, 21.
[55]Ibid., 86.

words, John the Baptist gave witness to the core meaning and reality of salvation – though he neither expressed it clearly nor in quite so explicit Trinitarian terms as Adrienne – that the Christ in some mysterious way, a way that Adrienne makes perfectly clear and understandable, already has His bride, the Immaculata. John the Baptist hinted at the Immaculate Conception, even placing it within a nuptial context, though he most likely did not understand the full impact of what he was prophesying.

With these points in mind, Adrienne also has something to say concerning the Son, the Immaculate Conception, and the Church.[56] In Adrienne's understanding the Immaculate Conception, as *event* and *person*, serves as the model and "prototype of the Church, the perfect bride in the ecclesial sense."[57] Christ's mission is to die for the sake of His *one* bride (Mary-Church); He does not have two brides. As a matter of fact, Christ *must* die for His Immaculate bride (Mary-Church) because if He does not, then we have an ontological problem due to the fact that the Virgin Mary has received the privilege of the Immaculate Conception in light of the merits of Christ's sacrifice on the Cross, and God's people (the Church) have been given divine promises of complete bridal renewal (immaculateness). Thus, the Immaculate Conception, the prototype of the bridal Church, is a sure proof that Christ will *necessarily* die on the Cross for His one bride; if the Immaculate Conception is from the Cross – and she is – then Christ *must* go there in order to redeem His one bride, Mary-Church.[58] In short, the reason

---

[56]For further reading in Speyrian/Balthasarian Mariological Ecclesiology see the work by Brendan Leahy, *The Marian Profile: In the Ecclesiology of Hans Urs von Balthasar* (New York: New City Press, 2000).

[57]von Speyr, *Mary in the Redemption*, 101.

[58]Following this general line of thought, Pope John Paul II recently stated that "the Immaculate Conception of the Virgin is a *pledge of salvation* for every human creature." See "For the Opening of the 150th Anniversary of the Immaculate Conception – Angelus Message," December 8, 2003. *L'Osservatore Romano*, English Edition, December 10, 2003; John Paul II also noted that "The Immaculate Conception is . . . the promising dawn of the radiant day of Christ." See "For the 12th World Day of the Sick, –

Christ came to die was to redeem the Immaculate – both Mary and the Church – and this is clearly shown through the truth of the Immaculate Conception, that is, the Immaculate Conception reveals the superabundant efficacy of Christ's sacrifice, for in His one sacrifice He both redeems the proto-type (The Immaculata) and that which is patterned off of her (The Church).

Continuing with this theme, and in order to root it in the sacred events of the life of Christ, Adrienne describes the agony of Jesus on the Mount of Olives as His full acceptance of the painful reality of the pre-redemption of His bride:

> There is a connection between Mary's pre-redemption in heaven and its acceptance on the Mount of Olives: her pre-redemption is com-pletely accepted on the Mount of Olives, and from there to the Cross its interest accrues until finally, with that interest, it is, as it were, subsumed in the paying of the price by the Son.[59]

Not only does Jesus redeem Mary and obtain for her the privilege of the Immaculate Conception, He also obtains for her the ability to objectively participate as Co-Redemptrix in His mission of salvation: "As God, he [Jesus] prepared the Mother's Immaculate Conception in secret, but he still has to pay the price of the Mother's earthly mission by suffering just as he pays the price of his own mission."[60] What this means is that Jesus will undergo His agony so that she can fully be the suf-fering Immaculate Co-Redemptrix and objectively participate with Him in the redemption of the world; it also signifies that Mary did not participate in the acquisition of the grace of her own Immaculate Conception, but, she, by the will of her divine Son, will have a share in the Son's obtaining all the other graces of redemption.[61]

---

11 February 2004 – Message to Cardinal Javier Lozano Barragán, President of the Pontifical Council for Health Pastoral Care," December 1, 2003. *L'Osservatore Romano*, English Edition, January 21, 2004.

[59]von Speyr, *Mary in the Redemption*, 76.

[60]Ibid., 75.

[61]A more detailed presentation of Adrienne's notion of the Immaculate Conception as Co-Redemptrix will be covered later in the paper.

Though it might at first appear that Adrienne is only speaking here about the Virgin Mary, it must be remembered that "whatever the Lord did for his Mother he did with his Church in mind."[62] For this reason Adrienne understands the inner form of the Church to be the Immaculate Conception: "She [Mary] was directly fashioned with regard to the Son's mission as the Immaculate Conception, for she is to make the Church possible, and the Son will not begin his work without the Church [His bride] being there in outline and in germ."[63] Adrienne at various places – far too numerous to note here – will even state that Mary *is* the Church: "the Mother of the Lord is the Church;"[64] and "the Church, in the first instance, means Mary herself."[65]

In making bold statements about Mary being the Church and Christ dying for her *necessarily*, it must be remembered that Christ has only one bride, Mary-Church. As Adrienne states: "The Lord turns his Mother into his bride, the Church."[66] All of this can only happen because Mary is the Immaculate Conception, the "inner immaculateness"[67] of the Church.[68] These two, Mary and the Church, form a unity due to the fact that, as was stated earlier: "whatever the Lord did to his Mother he did with his Church in mind."[69] The earthly Church will always have sinful members but as Adrienne states: "All the Church's short-comings, her inadequacies, faults, and blemishes, are, however, dissolved in the immaculate being of the virginal Bride."[70]

---

[62]von Speyr, *Handmaid of the Lord*, 139.

[63]Adrienne von Speyr, *The Cross: Word and Sacrament*. Trans. Graham Harrison. (San Francisco: Ignatius Press, 1983), 33-34.

[64]von Speyr, *Mary in the Redemption*, 95.

[65]von Speyr, *Handmaid of the Lord*, 139.

[66]von Speyr, *Mary in the Redemption*, 111.

[67]von Speyr, *Handmaid of the Lord*, 142.

[68]Pope John Paul II, in a homily given on December 8, 1985 to the Extraordinary Synod of Bishops, noted that it is through the "prism of the Immaculate Conception" that the Church comes to understand itself more fully. See *The Extraordinary Synod – 1985: Message to the People of God*. (Boston: Daughters of St. Paul, 1986), 97.

[69]von Speyr, *Handmaid of the Lord*, 139.

[70]von Speyr, *The Countenance of the Father*, 99-100.

For Adrienne, then, the Immaculate Conception is intimately bound up with Christology, Soteriology, and Ecclesiology. She seems to have an uncanny ability to bring all of these distinct theological fields into one admirable whole, causing new insights to emerge from her integrating approach. A perfect example of this emerges when we try and encapsulate the way in which she interconnects the Immaculata with the Church. One possible way of summing it up – though Adrienne never stated it as such – would be in the following terse statement: *immaculata facta ecclesia*. Naturally this calls to mind the ancient Franciscan axiom: *virgo facta ecclesia*. While both statements are certainly true, it would certainly seem that understanding the Church as being modeled after the Immaculate takes the ancient adage a step further. Was this not what St. Maximilian Kolbe, a faithful son of St. Francis, wanted to do? Surely it was. After all, it is the Holy Spirit and St. Paul who state that the Church is to be "without spot or wrinkle, or any such thing . . . holy and without blemish [immaculate]" (Eph.5:27).

c) The Holy Spirit & The Immaculate Conception

In considering the role of the Holy Spirit in relation to the mystery of the Immaculate Conception, Adrienne will once again place the overall theme within a Trinitarian context, especially emphasizing the dynamic synergy between the Father and the Holy Spirit who work together to present this gift, the Immaculate Conception, to the Son:

> Now it is fitting that, from the outset, the Father and the Holy Spirit show to the Son the efficacy of the Cross. In this regard, Mary is from the beginning a gift made by the Father and the Holy Spirit to the Son, almost as if the Mother, in her instrumentality, signified a form of pre-gift or deposit. In pre-redeeming the Mother toward the Cross (which ultimately means from the Cross), the Father and the Holy Spirit show to the Son the suitableness of the path upon which he has struck.[71]

---

[71]von Speyr, *Mary in the Redemption*, 17.

As can be seen, the Immaculate Conception is not only a gift to the Son from the Father but also a gift from the Holy Spirit to the Son. Yet, because the Father and the Sprit are distinct divine persons, Adrienne will acknowledge there to be a distinct role played by the Holy Spirit in relation to the Immaculate Conception, namely, an ongoing action that allows Mary to keep her immaculateness:

> The Spirit, who bears the seed of the Father into the womb of the Mother, accompanies this pre-redeemed Mother throughout her entire life. He receives her, as it were, from the Father's hands so as to give her back into these hands. He participates as her advocate and comforter by keeping her away from all sin.[72]

From this perspective, the relation of the Holy Spirit to the Immaculate Conception, both as *event* and as *person*, is not seen as a static relation. On the contrary, the Holy Spirit is the constant companion of the Immaculata, keeping her safe from all spiritual harm (original sin and personal sin). Fr. Jacques Servais, a noted Speyrian and Balthasarian scholar, makes reference to this Speyrian theme by stating the following: "The privilege conferred on her [Mary] by the Holy Spirit in prevision of the merits of Christ, her Immaculate Conception, must not be understood as a simple result of the redemption, but rather as the effectual power of fruitfulness."[73] This 'effectual power of fruitfulness' has its roots in the Trinity and makes its way to Mary through the conferral of grace; it is the work of the Holy Spirit to confer the fullness of grace upon the *event* and the *person* of the Immaculate Conception. For this reason, Adrienne can state that along with the Father and the Son, it is "the Spirit . . . who plays such a great role in the Immaculate Conception."[74] The Holy Spirit is the one who was, and is, constantly "overshadowing" both the person and mission of the Immaculata.

---

[72] Ibid., 18.

[73] Jacques Servais, "Mary's Role in the Incarnation," *Communio: International Catholic Review* 30 (Spring, 2003): 20.

[74] von Speyr, *Mary in the Redemption*, 86.

2) The Mission of the Immaculata

Another of Adrienne's ingenious insights into the Immaculate Conception, and Our Lady in general, concerns approaching the subject from the perspective of mission. Approaching the mystery of the Immaculate Conception from this vantage point affords us new insights into who Mary is as a 'person-in-mission' within salvation history (past, present, future). Anyone who has read Adrienne's works knows very well that her particular insights into the notion of mission occupy a central place in her overall thought.[75] Specifically, in regard to the Immaculate Conception, she seems to highlight two dimensions of mission: 1) The Immaculate Conception: Commencement of Our Lady's Mission, 2) The Annunciation: Revelation of Mission & Personal Assent.

a) The Immaculate Conception: Commencement of Our Lady's Mission

In order to begin this difficult exposition of Adrienne's thought on the Immaculate Conception it seems appropriate to let Adrienne speak for herself:

> The end is contained in the beginning; therefore it is included in the same surrender, and it resembles the beginning in that it is just as obscure. Of both the end and beginning [of her mission] one does not deep down know what they are in their inner essence, or when precisely they occur. The angel's visit seems to be a beginning and the death [of Christ] on the Cross, an end. But both are only the external event whereby something becomes visible which stretches out much farther in both directions [past and future]. The Mother

[75]The task of this section of the paper is not to present a theological analysis of either of her notions of person or mission; such a task would require a separate investigation. For those interested in this topic, the following works should be consulted: Hans Urs von Balthasar, *Theo-Drama, Theological Dramatic Theory. III. Dramatis Personae: Persons in Christ*. Trans. Graham Harrison. (San Francisco: Ignatius Press, 1992), esp. pp. 149-271; Robert Sokolowski, *Eucharistic Presence: A Study in the Theology of Disclosure*. (Washington, D.C.: Catholic University of America Press, 1994), esp. chapter 10 "The Christian Understanding of the Person," pp.118-137.

already said Yes before she began to pray, and this first prayer was already founded on her Immaculate Conception, which has its origin in the eternity of God.[76]

What this rather enigmatic statement describes, while being situated within the larger context of the Annunciation and Calvary, is that Mary's mission of cooperation in the redemption began with her Immaculate Conception, and continues even after the death of her Son. Adrienne will emphasize that even though the Immaculate Conception is a completely gratuitous gift from God, it is, also, the commencement of her mission because from the very beginning of her existence she is completely possessed by God, that is, full of grace. In other words, the mission of the Immaculata did not begin at the Annunciation. Rather, hers is a "mission which she received at the beginning"[77] – the Annunciation, as we will see in the next section, is the making visible (revelation), through personal assent, the mission which she already possesses due to her immaculate being (conception).

At this point, it is important to underscore what Adrienne is *not* saying about the Immaculate Conception and her mission. Adrienne, in seeking to highlight the fact that Mary's mission begins with her Immaculate Conception (and not at the Annunciation), is not stating that Mary somehow anticipates, goes before, her Immaculate Conception. Such an understanding would be unorthodox – it would imply that Mary existed before the Immaculate Conception.[78] Rather, what Adrienne seeks to emphasize by stating that Mary's mission begins with the Immaculate Conception is the idea that the Immaculate Conception contains within it a fundamental, ontological stance toward God, and though freely given by God as grace, a *fiat-structure* constitutes the essence of her being; in other words, once the Immaculate Conception occurs as *event* (grace freely

---

[76]von Speyr, *Handmaid of the Lord*, 118.

[77]Ibid., 28.

[78]That the Immaculate Conception has its origin in the eternity of God does not mean that the Immaculate Conception is divine. It simply means that it has been known by God, and planned by God, from all eternity.

given), the *person* of the Immaculata stands in relation to God as complete 'Yes', complete availability to His will. Adrienne underscores this element in a section where she expounds on Mary's prayer as a youth:

> She [Mary] is endowed with an attitude of prayer which is so much a part of her nature and an expression of her orientation to God that it is hers long before she can speak, long before she knows God. It is the attitude of the immaculate child, open to everything which presents itself to her and, since she is not touched by original sin, apprehending things with a great seriousness and an unclouded mind.[79]

Mary will certainly grow more fully into her mission, but the Immaculata's 'Yes' is there from the beginning because it is part of her being – it is at the Annunciation that her mission will appear visible and tangible (incarnational), and her already-existing Yes concrete (divine motherhood).

All of Mary's life is to be seen as pure continuity from one event to the next; in other words, there is no radical re-orienting of her life due to the fact that she only experienced one radical (root) direction in life: to be a theological person, a person-in-mission,[80] from the first moment of her grace-filled conception.[81] Thus, as Adrienne will state: "Her life runs along a

---

[79]Adrienne von Speyr, *The World of Prayer*, Trans. Graham Harrison. (San Francisco: Ignatius Press, 1985), 97.

[80]See von Balthasar, *Our Task*, 111.

[81]The Immaculate Conception is the reason for the pure continuity existing between all of Mary's various roles. Adrienne will explain this in regard to Mary's simultaneous spousal relation to God and St. Joseph: "That Mary perceives no contradiction or tension between surrender to God and surrender to her husband can only be understood in light of her Immaculate Conception." See *Handmaid of the Lord*, 54. Furthermore, it is interesting to note that von Balthasar, relying heavily upon Scheeben and von Speyr, grounds the paradoxical mission of the Immaculata, that is, her mission to be both the Mother and Companion-Bride of Christ, in a pre-lapsarian theological anthropology. In other words, she will only be able to fulfill her two-fold mission – maternal mediation and bridal co-suffering – if she is created in sanctifying grace, that is, the Immaculate Conception. The Immaculate Conception, for von Balthasar, takes away

straight path, without detours, which leads from the Immaculate Conception to the betrothal, to assent to the angel, to the Nativity and to the Cross. In this she shows that she is not subject to the law of original sin."[82] More precisely, the fact that she was immaculately conceived (grace-filled) has profound ontological implications. All who have come into the life of sanctifying grace (the inner life of the Trinity) have had a fundamental shift, an ontological jolt, in their orientation: 'being-out-of-grace' to 'being-in-grace'. Mary did not experience this ontological shift.[83]

Mary was conceived in sanctifying grace because of the loftiness of her mission, that is, to be the sinless (immaculate) handmaid of the Lord. Thus, Adrienne again brings out the ontological implications for Mary, the immaculate handmaid:

> When a person who has been tainted with original sin places himself, body and soul, at God's disposal, it never happens without a certain calculation. He sees and feels the renunciation of a great many natural gifts to which his nature seems to have a certain right, and what he has renounced is always reflected in his surrender. He cannot perfectly free himself from an attachment to what he has given away. The Mother [Mary] does not know this compromise. She does not weigh what she is giving and what she will receive for it. She knows no other use for her soul and body than being a servant.[84]

Mary's entire constitution (spirit, soul, body) is so radically oriented toward God "because she is the Immaculate Conception," that, as Adrienne notes, she "is thereby prepared to place herself thus at God's disposal."[85] Once again, this

---

the "tension" of how she can be both Mother and Bride of Christ. See von Balthasar, *Theo-Drama III. Dramatis Personae: Persons in Christ.* pp.318-327.

[82]von Speyr, *Handmaid of the Lord*, 56.

[83]Pope John Paul II stated it this way: "The unique privilege of the Immaculate Conception influenced the whole development of the young woman of Nazareth's spiritual life." *Theotókos: Woman, Mother, Disciple.* (Boston: Pauline Books & Media, 2000), 118.

[84]von Speyr, *Handmaid of the Lord*, 15-16.

[85]Ibid., 16.

should not lead us to conclude that Mary did not grow into her mission; Adrienne affirms that Mary was a free creature, undergoing with all human creatures a development – as the Second Vatican Council called it, a "pilgrimage of faith."[86] Thus the Immaculate Conception *as mission* should be understood as the "seed" which contains the entire fruit, while, at the same time, allowing for natural and necessary growth and development.[87] As Adrienne states: "A mission is not only something to be received and completed once and for all. It is also something growing, something to be newly undertaken and affirmed every day. Mary is always receiving her mission anew from the Son, all the way to the Cross."[88]

One last point that needs to be mentioned concerning Adrienne's notion of the Immaculate Conception as mission is that it only takes on meaning in light of the mission of Christ: "The loftiness of the Mother's mission lies in its being a mission in the Son. Every Christian mission is contained in the mission of the Lord: it has its origin in him."[89] Thus, the mission of the Immaculata, as in all Christian missions, is Christo-form. Nevertheless, in the mind of Adrienne, there does exist a certain paradox in the fact that the Son allows His mission to be built upon, and even become dependent upon, the mission of the Immaculata.

Concerning this wondrous inter-dependence of missions, Adrienne will note: "Mary's mission paves the way for the Son's mission. In accepting him [in the Incarnation], she accepts his mission within herself. Nonetheless, her mission is included in his to such an extent that he would sever his very self were he to sever himself from the Mother's mis-

[86]*Lumen Gentium*, 58.
[87]St. Maximilian Kolbe taught something similar: "Every man is born with the capacities required for the mission which God intends to entrust to him." See Manteau-Bonamy, *Immaculate Conception and the Holy Spirit*, 57.
[88]von Speyr, *Handmaid of the Lord*, 47.
[89]Adrienne von Speyr, *The Mission of the Prophets*, Trans. David Kipp. (San Francisco: Ignatius Press, 1996), 123.

sion."[90] Adrienne will even state that Mary is "an inseparable element of the mission of the Son himself."[91] This mutual interpenetration and dependence of missions between the Immaculate Mother and the Divine Son is truly a work of the God of paradox!

b) The Annunciation: Revelation of Mission & Personal Assent

As was already stated, Adrienne understands Mary's mission to reside in both the *event* and the *person* of the Immaculate Conception. The Immaculate Conception remains both the gratuitous gift of God and the preparation for the climactic *fiat* that will bring about the instrument of our salvation, namely, the flesh of the God-man. After all, if God would prepare from the womb such a prophet as Jeremiah – a prophet whose mission was to utter the word of God – how much more would God radically (root) prepare the one who was to bear His Word and bring Him into the world! All of the preparations of the past, whether in prophets or Old Testament figures, pale in comparison to the radical preparation that God would fashion for the one who was to be the Mother of His Son and prototype of the Church: the Immaculata.

Mary, as the Immaculate Conception, is in mission from the first moment of her existence because of the primacy of God's grace. She will grow into her mission by coming to know it more fully, but the form her mission will take – the concrete aspect of her mission – she leaves for God to reveal to her. As the Immaculata, she accepts all things and awaits further instruction from the One to whom she makes herself pure availability. Once again this points back to her fundamental stance as handmaid. She has complete trust in God and knows that in His time he will reveal to her the concrete direction of her life. From this perspective we can see that the

---

[90] von Speyr, *Mary in the Redemption*, 76.
[91] von Speyr, *Handmaid of the Lord*, 49.

Annunciation does not come out of nowhere; it has a history and a preparation. Adrienne will state this fact quite clearly:

> The angel shows Mary her situation; he does not create it. Through the greeting she achieves possession of self-knowledge; but she herself seems in this to be standing already in the service of heaven. The salutation sounds like a retrospect of her entire attitude until now, and we are not told when her mission had begun. The greeting promises a coming event; she is going to conceive the Son, she does not yet have him physically in her. But her mission she possesses already; it is much older than the conception [of Jesus]. And so the promise of the Lord who is to come is the verification of the Lord who is already there in the mission which she received at the beginning [the Immaculate Conception].[92]

In this profoundly insightful statement, we note the importance of looking at the Annunciation through the lens of the Immaculate Conception – without the reality of the Immaculate Conception there could be no Annunciation.[93] In essence, in Adrienne's thought, the Annunciation requires that Mary be already in mission, a mission stemming from her being the Immaculata and already responding to God through complete availability, something only she can do because only she possesses the privilege of having the integrity consonant with being the Immaculate Conception.[94] In no way, however, should her already existing as a theological person in mission before the event of the Annunciation lead us to minimize the importance of her assent at the Annunciation; on the contrary, the Immaculate Conception and the *fiat* uttered at the Annunciation are inseparably linked. As Adrienne will state: "As a sheaf of grain is tied

[92]Ibid., 28.

[93]The *Catechism of the Catholic Church* emphatically affirms this point: "In fact, in order for Mary to be able to give the free assent of her faith to the announcement of her vocation, it was necessary that she be wholly borne of God's grace." par. 490.

[94]For example, as the Immaculate Conception, she would possess the seven gifts of the Holy Spirit, the infused theological and moral virtues, and complete integrity between spirit, soul and body.

together in the middle and spreads out at either end, so Mary's life is bound together by her assent [at the Annunciation].[95]

The Annunciation is where the mission of the Immaculata becomes visible, where it is fully revealed. To reveal something does not mean that that which is revealed did not previously exist, as if revelation were synonymous with creation. On the contrary, when a 'revelation' occurs it always implies that what is being revealed had prior existence and is now being given (revealed or unveiled) for the sake of direction – revelation is never static. At the Annunciation the Immaculata gives her climactic *fiat* to her already existent mission because at the announcement of the angel her mission takes on real (incarnational) direction: she is to be Mother of the God-man. Furthermore, the fact that Mary is the Immaculate Conception is the *sine qua non* for her full and freely given *fiat* in response to the angel. In the following passage Adrienne succinctly states the interrelatedness between the Immaculate Conception as mission and the personal assent of the Immaculata at the Annunciation:

> . . . at the moment of her conception she was dissociated from original sin and thus from everything that might have weakened or impaired in her the power and perfection of her later assent. So great is the power and freedom of her consent that she is perfectly free from the slightest inclination to say No. This is so because her assent is prepared and planned from the first moment of her existence.[96]

Thus, the primacy of grace – evident in the gratuitousness of the Immaculate Conception – is at the foundations of both the Immaculate Conception and the Incarnation (Mary's assent to God's plan of salvation). Grace gives the freedom that allows one to be available for the purposes of God – where there is no grace there is no freedom. For this reason, the Immaculata knows full well that the privilege of being the

[95]von Speyr, *Handmaid of the Lord*, 7.
[96]Ibid.

Mother of God does not rely solely upon her personal assent. As Adrienne will note:

> Assent, in its essence, is grace; a grace which, like every grace, comes from God, takes effect in man and his mission and has the possibility of being sent back autonomously, as a formed answer incorporated within the all-embracing mission of the Son, who, through the assent of man, then has the possibility of coming into the world as man.[97]

As the Immaculate Conception Mary cooperates with God in His saving plan, but she is also always aware that her cooperation as humble handmaid is meant to serve the greater mystery of the Incarnation:

> Because she is the Immaculate Conception and therefore has herself a wonderful mystery in her own origin, for that very reason she steps back completely before the greater mystery of her Son's birth. Not because she is so great as the Immaculately Conceived does God choose her for his mother, but rather, to put it plainly, in spite of the fact that she was already so much the Elect, she still performs this highest act of obedience by becoming the Mother of the Lord.[98]

Furthermore, according to Adrienne, the assent of the humble and obedient Immaculate handmaid is so important that it becomes not only the cradle of Christ, but, also the "cradle of all Christianity."[99] The Immaculata is always at the service of humanity and its coming to know the God-man, Jesus Christ, because the Immaculata is always at the service of the Incarnate One. As the Immaculate Mother, through her free assent, she becomes the "refuge and protectress of mankind."[100] Thus the *fiat* of the Immaculata, because it is the "condition and proto-type, indeed the source, of all Christian assent to come,"[101] has a universal (catholic) dimension, which means that no one is exempt from going to Jesus through Mary.

[97]Ibid., 11.
[98]Ibid., 26
[99]Ibid., 68.
[100]Ibid., 140.
[101]Ibid., 11-12.

3) Immaculate Co-Redemptrix

When we investigate Adrienne's understanding of Mary's role as Co-Redemptrix, we are immediately brought back to the privilege of her Immaculate Conception. The reasons for this should be obvious from what we have already presented, namely, since Mary's mission began with her Immaculate Conception her role as Co-Redemptrix also began there. Thus, as Adrienne notes, Mary "was Co-Redemptrix before she spoke her personal Yes."[102] This is an insight into Mary's role as Co-Redemptrix because many thinkers tend to posit that her role as Co-Redemptrix only began at the Annunciation.[103] Yet, if all of Mary's privileges were already present as capacities in the event of the Immaculate Conception – due to the loftiness and gratuity of her mission – then from the beginning she is the Immaculate Co-Redemptrix.

Adrienne does posit, however, that if Mary is to fulfill the role of Co-Redemptrix concretely, that is, real, meritorious co-suffering with Christ, she must have an unparalleled preparation;[104] this preparation is the completely free gift of her Immaculate Conception, and Mary can only be Co-Redemptrix because of it:

> A purification without personal guilt has to be a purification for God to dispose of as he desires. In this Mary becomes Co-Redemptrix.

[102]von Speyr, *Mary in the Redemption*, 26.

[103]For example, since many of the early Church Fathers, especially the eastern Fathers, knew that Mary played a role in the redemption as associate and helpmate of Christ, they would often claim that Mary had to undergo some type of purification in order to participate in such an exalted role. Due to their inability to fully understand Mary's sanctity (sinlessness), they usually attributed a form of pre-purification, *procatharsis*, to the event of the Annunciation. See Manuel Candal, S.J. "La Virgen Santisima 'prepurificada' en su Anunciación," *Orientalia Christiana Periodica* 31 (1965): 241-276.

[104]Adrienne will employ the language of 'purification' to describe this preparation, but in no way does she mean that Mary was at any time under the bondage of sin, whether original or personal.

> This is not because she had to earn the grace of being the one who is pre-redeemed at the Cross. Her suffering is not used for that. It is free from the outset. She does not become one who is pre-redeemed through the co-redemption, but rather she becomes Co-Redemptrix through the pre-redemption [her Immaculate Conception]. The pre-redemption [Immaculate Conception] is a completely free gift of grace from God that serves as the prerequisite for everything else.[105]

For Adrienne the terminology of pre-redemption is synonymous with the event of the Immaculate Conception and gives witness to the primacy and gratuity of God's grace. The gift of Mary's pre-redemption, the privilege of the Immaculate Conception, is the radical preparation so that she might be able to fulfill her lofty mission of being Co-Redemptrix. In this sense, as Adrienne will state, "her co-redemption [role as Co-Redemptrix] was already planned and contained in her pre-redemption [Immaculate Conception]."[106]

This should not lead us, however, to dismiss the power, efficacy, and merit of the "co-redemptive fiat"[107] uttered by Mary at the Annunciation. As was stated earlier, Mary's entire immaculate being is nothing but availability to the will of God. There is no radical shift in Mary's mission; the continuity of her role as Immaculate Co-Redemptrix is seen in all stages of her life. Thus, although the Annunciation scene does not commence Mary's role as Co-Redemptrix but, rather, serves as a 'revelation' and further instruction as to the concrete (incarnational) path her role as Immaculate Co-Redemptrix will take, nonetheless, the Annunciation is of paramount importance for salvation.

Another aspect to Adrienne's understanding of Mary's role as Co-Redemptrix is the fact that it is only because Mary is the Immaculate Conception that she can be an immaculate, meritorious victim and co-sufferer with Christ. Concerning this, Adrienne will state:

---

[105]von Speyr, *Mary in the Redemption*, 80.
[106]Ibid., 83-84.
[107]See von Speyr, *Handmaid of the Lord*, 67.

> She [Mary] stands before the Lord on the Cross like the embodi-
> ment and summation of mankind. When he looks at her, he no
> longer sees, for a moment, the atrocious sinners for whose sake
> and at whose hands he is dying; he sees mankind as if transfig-
> ured in the form of his Mother. He had redeemed her also, by pre-
> serving her from sin. That gives her the capacity to suffer with him,
> vicariously for all, as an embodiment of the meaning of redemption,
> in the perfect unity of human nature and divine grace.[108]

Due to the close collaboration in which the Son pre-
redeemed Mary in order to associate her "necessarily in his act
of redemption"[109] Adrienne will posit that "Mary has real merit
in the redemption."[110] Naturally Mary's form of merit would be
de congruo (from fittingness), while Christ's would be *de
condigno* (from dignity) but, nevertheless, it is real merit in the
redemption.[111]

Furthermore, it is because Mary is immaculate that she
can participate in the redemption of mankind as Co-
Redemptrix, co-suffering victim with Christ. According to
Adrienne's thought Mary "does not have the "alleviation" of
original sin, which covers so much for the sinner. She is completely unprotected and exposed."[112] Thus, her Immaculate
Conception gives her the ability to suffer perfectly and freely,
entering into the passion as pure victim. Adrienne will also, in
no uncertain terms, elaborate upon the real, painful participato-
ry sacrifice made by the Immaculate Conception in the
redemption of mankind:

> It will be much harder for the Son to take her, the innocent, with
> him into his Passion and to make use of her purity in a way that

---

[108]Ibid., 116-117.

[109]Ibid., 37.

[110]Ibid.

[111]A classical understanding of these notions is the distinction between
objective and subjective redemption. It can be said that Jesus and Mary
alone (Mary, of course, in a subordinate sense) participate in objective
redemption, i.e., both the acquisition and distribution of the graces of
redemption; the Church participates only in subjective redemption, i.e.,
the distribution of the graces of redemption.

[112]von Speyr, *Handmaid of the Lord*, 122.

involves her in the work of redemption and makes her Co-Redemptrix. It will be much harder to involve one who is immaculate in all this than a convert, who has many personal things to atone and therefore gladly cooperates in bearing a share of the common guilt. The sacrificing of the Mother here approaches the killing of the "innocents".[113]

Another point is that Mary's exalted role, always understood by Adrienne in nuptial categories,[114] manifests her "feminine role as co-redemptrix."[115] Therefore, the Immaculata becomes the model for the bridal co-redeeming Church since she is the "one who was pre-redeemed and who became the Church."[116] In this sense, Adrienne has the perfect blend of Christo-typical Mariology (Mary's relation to Christ) and Ecclesio-typical Mariology (Mary's relation to the Church), as indicated in the following passage:

> The Son needs the Mother's suffering: not to lessen his own, but so that his suffering can begin to be affirmed and taken up by the other believers, so that it can be completed and spread abroad in the Church, according to his predetermined plan. The Mother's Yes, her consent, uttered and lived out, was essential: it was to be an archetype, an example making [co-redemptive] suffering possible for the whole Church.[117]

There are some statements that Adrienne makes concerning the relation between Mary's Immaculate Conception and her role as Co-Redemptrix that must be understood within the totality of her overall thought. For example, in a rather lengthy passage, Adrienne offers profound speculative insights into this topic:

---

[113]von Speyr, *Mary in the Redemption*, 32.
[114]It is worth noting that in the foreword to the Italian translation of *Mary in the Redemption*, Roberto Carelli underscores Adrienne's notion of Mary Co-Redemptrix as a nuptial role. See Adrienne von Speyr, *Maria nella Redenzione*, Trans. Roberto Carelli. (Milano: Jaca Books, 2001), 7-23.
[115]von Speyr, *Handmaid of the Lord*, 72.
[116]von Speyr, *Mary in the Redemption*, 109.
[117]Adrienne von Speyr, *Three Women and the Lord*. Trans. Graham Harrison (San Francisco: Ignatius Press, 1986), 27.

She [Mary] exists in such harmony with corrected creation that redemption needs her as Co-Redemptrix. And, since redemption is the establishing of the true creature, being co-redeemed cannot be detached from co-creation. Of course, Mary is not there on the day of the first creation. But she is given the role of co-creating at the point at which it concerns the correction of creation and the restoration of Eve. In order to be capable of this, she is born without original sin in the same grace that Adam and Eve possessed before they fell, thus in the same grace that the Son possesses as Redeemer and in which he allows his Mother to participate. But in order to let her really become Co-Redemptrix, he must already distribute her being throughout the Old Testament. He does not simply want to return to Adam in himself, but also to Eve in Mary. Man alone should not be the one who is redeeming and redeemed: woman, too, should be the first redeemed and therefore co-redeeming. Just as Adam and Eve have sinned with one another, so, too, must the Son and Mother, at another level, redeem with one another; they put the work of redemption into place where the fall from sin occurred. Eve drew Adam into sin, and Christ draws Mary into redemption.[118]

This passage is as theologically profound as it is long! Yet, in all simplicity it is nothing more than a return to understanding redemption in classical Irenaen categories of recapitulation and recirculation. Certainly Adrienne takes it a step further by her insinuation – for she never stated it as such – that Mary is not only "causa salutis" but also "causa creationis".[119] In another lengthy passage, Adrienne elaborates upon this:

Mary, the pre-redeemed, is already active as the one planned by God. In this respect, she forms a unique encounter between creation and (pre)-redemption [Immaculate Conception]. A human father can say, "I want my son to be a doctor. From the day he was born I've done everything I can to make sure it happens." But the son is

---

[118]von Speyr, *Mary in the Redemption*, 64-65.

[119]Interestingly, John Paul II recently noted: "The Dogma of the Immaculate Conception introduces us into the heart of the mystery of the Creation and Redemption." See "For the 12th World Day of the Sick, 11 February, 2004 – Message to Cardinal Javier Lozano Barragán, President of the Pontifical Council for Health Pastoral Care," December 1, 2003. *L'Osservatore Romano*, English Edition, January 21, 2004.

of course always free to do something else. When, however, God the Father begins with Mary and her pre-redemption [Immaculate Conception], the realization of his plan already exists, so to speak. It is absolutely certain that she will henceforth belong to heaven and that her place there was secured from its creation. She is not pre-redeemed in a mere image or idea, but in fact and reality. It is a fact with real consequences. In eternal life such concrete certainties do exist. Accordingly, something of her already existed at the creation of the world. Her characteristics do not float around unpossessed, but rather she possesses them from the beginning. She has her place in the course of the world's creation precisely because of her function as "Co-Redemptrix". The idea of "co-redemption" is "older" than that of the pre-redemption: the latter is a consequence of the former, a means to an end.[120]

From this perspective Mary, as Immaculate Co-Redemptrix, is the original (first) plan of God for creation, thus Adrienne considers Mary to be the "first Eve"[121] who was "co-redeeming from eternity".[122] Therefore, since Mary is in some sense a cause of both creation and salvation, Adrienne understands her to be the "mediatrix of all graces"[123] and the "nodal point at which all graces run together."[124] These statements should not lead us to conclude that Adrienne is positing divinity to Mary, or stating that Mary existed before her Immaculate Conception. On the contrary, Adrienne's main point is that the Immaculate Co-Redemptrix serves as the prototype of all creation and salvation; and because of this, she "goes before" – in the eternal mind of God – all finite things.

Perhaps returning to the theme of Mary as the 'first Eve' might help us to understand exactly what Adrienne means in the above statements:

Assume that a sculptor has a block of marble. Because the block has a certain form, he decides to shape the statue in a certain way.

---

[120] von Speyr, *Mary in the Redemption*, 19.

[121] Ibid., 20.

[122] Ibid., 112

[123] Ibid., 86, 107, 108.

[124] Ibid., 57.

He will get to work on the statue, however, only once he has made a model out of ordinary clay of what he has in mind. Although the shape of the stone played a part in determining the idea, which is now exact in his mind, he will get to work on the marble only once he has made the clay model. In relation to Eve, Mary is the piece of marble that was there from the start.[125]

The logic used here by Adrienne also applies to her understanding of how Mary can be both the *causa creationis et salutis*, namely, Mary as mere creature – in contrast to the hypostatic union in the divine person of Jesus Christ, which is a marriage between divinity (God) and humanity (man) – serves as the blueprint of all finite (created) things, and this because of the privilege of her Immaculate Conception.

Conclusion

All in all, the thought of Adrienne von Speyr on the Blessed Virgin Mary, in particular, Mary's privilege of the Immaculate Conception, provides current Mariological studies with much by way of new theological and mystical insights. In some mysterious way, Adrienne is able to combine Catholic Tradition, doctrine, and magisterial teaching on Mary in such a way that the insights of the past ages are firmly held, and the new insights, while not only remaining simply rooted in the wisdom of the past, build on it and resonate harmoniously in order to present a fuller image of both the event and the person of the Immaculate Conception. A blend such as this, deeply theological and, at the same time, intensely devotional, is a gift for the Church in an age when theology and spirituality (holiness) are often presented in institutions of higher learning as fiercely inimical. A return to presenting Mary authentically in both theological circles as well as pious associations is certainly what is needed today. Adrienne offers such a solution.

What is perhaps the most interesting facet of Adrienne's insights into the Immaculate Conception is that she bridges the

[125] Ibid., 20.

chasm that can often occur in Mariology when too much emphasis is placed on one of two approaches, namely, Christo-typical or Ecclesio-typical Mariology. After Vatican Council II a serious rift occurred between these two approaches, often resulting in a neglect of the Christo-typical stance – although the papacy of John Paul II has sought to correct this aberration. Adrienne, for her part, knew of no such distinctions; she presents Mary, the Immaculate Conception, as necessarily related to both Christ *and* the Church. To overemphasize one will ultimately lead to the degradation of the other. Her genius is that she so integrates the two – something she does without even being aware of it – that she presents her readers with a tension-less Mariology, something rare in post-Vatican II Mariology.

Furthermore, her Trinitarian approach is truly fascinating when one considers the implications of her thought. By placing the mystery of the Immaculate Conception within a Trinitarian framework, Adrienne has given modern Mariologists much to ponder; for this reason her insights into the Blessed Virgin Mary could be classified as part of the mid-twentieth century *ressourcement* approach. In addition, her profound insights into the nature of the mission of the Immaculata, that is, when the Immaculata's mission began and what it requires to be completed, are insights that will surely gloss the pages of theologians and Mariologists for centuries to come.

The twentieth century was given a great gift in the person and ecclesial mission of Adrienne von Speyr. In can only be hoped that soon all of her works will be translated and studied in greater depth. Ultimately, what Adrienne has to say to the Church and to the world concerning Mary's Immaculate Conception is that it is a privilege given both for Mary and for us, *pro nobis*. For, as Adrienne stated so well: "The protection of Mary from original sin is, for all of us, an invitation to purity, the grace of redemption, and the mystery of the Cross."[126]

---

[126]von Speyr, *The Countenance of the Father*, 97.

THE IMMACULATE CONCEPTION
AND THE CO-REDEMPTRIX

Mark I. Miravalle, S.T.D.

On February 17, 1941, the "Property" of the Immaculata, Fr. Maximilian Kolbe, was arrested by the Nazi Gestapo, eventually leading to his martyrdom in Auschwitz. During the few hours before his arrest, Fr. Maximilian was inspired to write the heart of his unparalleled Mariological ponderings regarding the "Immaculate Conception."

The following are excerpts from this last written testimony:

> IMMACULATE CONCEPTION: These words fell from the lips of the Immaculata herself. Hence, they must tell us in the most precise and essential manner who she really is.

> Since human words are incapable of expressing divine realities, it follows that these words: "Immaculate," and "Conception" must be understood in a much more beautiful and sublime meaning than usual: a meaning beyond that which human reason at its most penetrating, commonly gives to them . . . Who then are you, O Immaculate Conception?

> Not God, of course, because he has no beginning. Not an angel, created directly out of nothing. Not Adam, formed out of the dust of the earth (Gen. 2:7). Not Eve, molded from Adam's rib (Gen. 2:21). Not the Incarnate Word, who exists before all ages, and of whom we should use the word "conceived" rather than "conception." Humans do not exist before their conception, so we might call them created "conception." But you, O Mary, are different from all other children of Eve. They are conceptions stained by original sin; whereas you are the unique Immaculate Conception.

Creatures, by following the natural law implanted in them by God, reach their perfection, become like him, and go back to him. Intelligent creatures love him in a conscious manner; through this love they unite themselves more and more closely with him, and so find their way back to him. The creature most completely filled with this love, with God himself, was the Immaculata, who never contracted the slightest stain of sin, who never departed in the least from God's will. United to the Holy Spirit as his spouse, she is one with God in an incomparably more perfect way than can be predicated of any other creature.

What sort of union is this? It is above all an interior union, a union of her essence with the "essence" of the Holy Spirit. The Holy Spirit dwells in her, lives in her. This was true from the first instance of her existence. It is always true; it will always be true.

In what does this life of the Spirit in Mary consist? He himself is uncreated Love in her; the Love of the Father and of the Son, the Love by which God loves himself, the very love of the Most Holy Trinity. He is a fruitful Love, a "Conception." Among creatures made in God's image the union brought about by married love is the most intimate of all (cf. Mt. 19:6). In a much more precise, more interior, more essential manner, the Holy Spirit lives in the soul of the Immaculata, in the depths of her very being. He makes her fruitful, from the very instance of her existence, all during her life, and for all eternity.

This eternal "Immaculate Conception" (which is the Holy Spirit) produces in an immaculate manner divine life itself in the womb (or depths) of Mary's soul, making her the Immaculate Conception, the human Immaculate Conception. And the virginal womb of Mary's body is kept sacred for him; there he conceives in time — because everything that is material occurs in time — the human life of the Man-God.[1]

In a 1933 Letter from Nagasaki, St. Maximilian explains further that in the name, "Immaculate Conception," the Mother also gives us the secret of her very nature:

In her apparition at Lourdes she does not say: "I was conceived immaculately," but "I am the Immaculate Conception." This points out not only the fact that she was conceived without original sin, but also the manner in which this privilege belongs to her.

[1] H. M. Manteau-Bonamy, O.P., *Immaculate Conception and the Holy Spirit: The Marian Teachings of St. Maximilian Kolbe*. (Libertyville: Franciscan Marytown Press, 1977), 1, 2, 4.

It is not something accidental; it is something that belongs to her very nature. For she is Immaculate Conception in [her very] person.[2]

The uncreated Immaculate Conception and the created Immaculate Conception. The Divine Spirit and the human spouse perfected in His grace are united by an interior, *essential* union. Uncreated love conceives and dwells within the depths of her soul, and she becomes His quasi-incarnation.[3] For this reason, as St. Maximilian tells us, Mary is also the Mediatrix of all graces and gifts of the Spirit:

The union between the Immaculata and the Holy Spirit is so inexpressible, yet so perfect, that the Holy Spirit acts only by the Most Blessed Virgin, his Spouse. This is why she is Mediatrix of all grace given by the Holy Spirit. And since every grace is a gift of God the Father through the Son and by the Holy Spirit, it follows that there is no grace which Mary cannot dispose of as her own, which is not given to her for this purpose.[4]

Does St. Maximilian go too far in speaking in this manner of the wonders of the Immaculate Conception? Or does he say too little? The Mariology disclosed by the saint of the Immaculata, generous and profound as it is, in no way exhausts the mystery of the Immaculate Conception. His unrivaled pneumatological discoveries prepare the way for a new comprehension of the inseparability of the Uncreated Immaculate Conception with the created Immaculate Conception. But the mystery continues. The brilliance of St. Maximilian's methodology in his return to Trinitarian Mariology specific to the Holy Spirit also propels us to ponder more deeply the other relationships of the Immaculata with her Triune God.

Perhaps least developed of these, from a Trinitarian perspective, is the relationship between the Immaculate Conception and the Heavenly Father. The Father-daughter

---

[2] St. Maximilian Kolbe, *Letter from Nagasaki to the Youth of the Franciscan Order*, February 28, 1933.
[3] Manteau-Bonamy, *Immaculate Conception and the Holy Spirit*, 63-64.
[4] St. Maximilian, *Letter to Father Mikolajczyk*, July 28, 1935.

relationship is one of the most precious of human relationships, and no other relationship captures more the love of the Creator for creation, and the appropriate reciprocal love of creation for the Creator than the relationship between the Eternal Father and Mary Immaculate. At the heart of this union of Perfect Daughter to Perfect Father, which represents and exemplifies how every creature should be united to its Creator, is the stainlessness and fullness of grace possessed by the Immaculate Daughter. *This "stainless-fullness" is given to her by the Eternal Father through the Spirit and in view of the foreseen merits of the Son, which is the foundation of her perfect response of fiat-love to everything given to her and asked of her by her "Abba," God the Father of all mankind.*

As the example of St. Maximilian makes clear, the dogmatic proclamation of the Immaculate Conception in 1854 does not end its doctrinal development, but rather encourages more unveiling and more appreciation of its sacred mystery. Certainly contemporary Mariology would do well to follow the example of St. Maximilian in striving to incorporate a more Trinitarian perspective and methodology in relation to the Blessed Virgin if we seek to be true to the full glory of Mary Immaculate.

We must seek to view Mary from the perspective of the Father, as the Virgin Daughter Immaculate, His greatest masterpiece. We must view Mary afresh from the perspective of the Son, as perfect Mother in the order of love, and most intimate partner and co-redeemer in the historic sufferings of Redemption. We must view Mary from the perspective of the Spirit, as His entirely pure and eternally faithful spouse, in a certain sense his "quasi-incarnation," and the Mediatrix of all of the Sanctifier's gifts to humanity. Only by seeking to comprehend the Immaculate One with the mind of the Trinity, and striving to love her through the heart of the Trinity, can we hope to do even partial justice to her.

Western Mariology must be on guard against the subtle tendency (even unconscious at times), to think first in terms of apologetics, rather than in terms of mystery. If the first question of our Mariological methodology is, "how can I explain this to someone who does not believe it?," rather than, "what is the depth and fullness of this revealed Marian mystery?," the resulting product will be a Marian minimalism, a "too summary an attitude" as the Council prohibits,[5] which will always fall short of what the human mind and heart should truly grasp with the help of grace about the Mother of the Word, who is God's climax of creation.

Here we see light from the East. The Eastern Church looks first to the transcendence of the all pure *Theotokos*, the "God-bearer," which it liturgically praises as the "ever holy, ever pure, ever blessed and glorious Lady."[6] In his 1998 Marian Lenten letter to the Orthodox world, the present Patriarch of Constantinople, Bartholomew I, writes:

> The Lady, the Virgin Mother, shines as the one who conceived joy for the world. She shines as the meaning of history; the goal of creation; She who made our composition heavenly ... She deliberately followed her Son, Himself God, from His Birth to His Passion and Cross. And the God-man from high on the Cross, sent forth His Most Holy Mother to all of us as our Mother in the order of grace.

> She supports our life and sanctifies our time ... We are purified through her tears; through the divine beauty we are saved; and we keep holy silence in the presence of the overwhelming awe.[7]

The inestimable magnitude of the Immaculata in her overflowing plentitude of divine grace (cf. Luke 1:28) and her absolute freedom from all sin (cf. Gen. 3:15), is described by Bl. Pius IX in *Ineffabilis Deus*:

---

[5] Second Vatican Council, *Lumen Gentium*, November 21, 1964, 67.[6]

[6] The Divine Liturgy of St. John Chrysostom.

[7] Ecumenical Patriarch Bartholomew I, *Universal Lenten Encyclical on the Mother of God and Mother of us All in the Order of Grace*, March 1998.

Therefore, far above all the angels and all the saints so wondrously did God endow her with the abundance of all heavenly gifts poured from the treasury of his divinity that this mother, ever absolutely free of all stain of sin, all fair and perfect, would possess that fullness of holy innocence and sanctity than which, under God, one cannot even imagine anything greater, and which, outside of God, no mind can succeed in comprehending fully.[8]

I.   "The Co-Redemptrix" Because "The Immaculate Conception"

The Immaculate Conception, the unparalleled prodigy of grace granted by the Eternal Father, is (along with her Divine Maternity), *the foundation for all of the subsequent roles assigned her by the Trinity for the benefit of humanity*.

Indeed, the humble Virgin of Nazareth is the Co-Redemptrix not only because she is Mother of God, but also because she is the Immaculate Conception. Stainless, full of grace, and in total enmity with Satan and his seed of evil and sin, the Immaculate One is created by the Father, in view of the merits of the Son, precisely to be the perfect human cooperator "with Jesus" in the historic work of human salvation.

Any sin on Mary's part, original or personal, would establish a bond or union between herself and Satan, the historic foe of the Redeemer. Mary, then, would become a type of "double-agent" — working with Jesus, but also having an association with his Adversary, the very person and power from which Jesus seeks to buy back humanity.

No, the woman chosen to be humanity's representative, to participate intimately and proximately with God Himself in restoring supernatural life to souls, must be without any union through sin with the Enslaver and Defiler of humanity. Thus was she created immaculate by God the Father of all mankind, crafted from incorruptible "wood" so as to be the

---

[8] Bl. Pius IX, Dogmatic Bull, *Ineffabilis Deus,* December 8, 1854.

New Ark of the New Covenant, carrying the Redeemer of the world in her immaculate womb and dying with Him in her immaculate heart for the Redemption of the world (cf. *Lumen Gentium* 58, 61).

Pope John Paul II teaches the essential relationship between the Immaculate Conception and Our Lady's coredemptive role with Jesus in salvation, and explains that her complete immunity from all sin allowed for the perfect fulfillment of this co-working role in Redemption:

> We must above all note that Mary was created immaculate in order to be better able to act on our behalf. The fullness of grace allowed her to fulfill perfectly her mission of collaboration with the work of salvation; it gave the maximum value to her cooperation in the sacrifice. When Mary presented to the Father her Son nailed to the cross, her painful offering was entirely pure.[9]

We do not seek mediation from one who is himself at odds with the person with whom we desire to be reconciled. We do not seek relief from a debt by asking assistance from someone who is himself in a state of debt to the person we owe.

This is why the Father in His infinite wisdom, in assigning to the Virgin Daughter the providential role of Co-Redemptrix and its consequential roles as Mediatrix of all graces and Advocate for all humanity, created her in full union with the Redeemer, with no association in any dimension with the Enemy, and in absolute segregation from sin. In this way, Mary Immaculate becomes the Co-Redemptrix with Jesus the Divine Redeemer in the historic work of Redemption, which indeed "buys us back" (*redimere* — to buy back). She becomes the Immaculate Mediatrix of all grace, who with the one Mediator "brings us the gifts of eternal salvation."[10] She becomes the all-pure Advocate who presents our petitions to our Divine Judge and King.

---

[9] John Paul II, December 7, 1983 Address, *L'Osservatore Romano*, English edition, December 12, 1983, p. 1.
[10] Cf. *Lumen Gentium*, 62.

There is yet another sense in which the Immaculate Conception brings clarity to Mary's coredemptive mission. The objection is sometimes raised, "How can Mary be Co-Redemptrix if she herself was in need of Redemption?"[11] The answer is found in a proper understanding of her Immaculate Conception.

Indeed, it is true that Mary needed to be "redeemed" for her own salvation, and in order to actively participate in the process of human Redemption for the rest of humanity.

In the papal definition of the Immaculate Conception, Bl. Pope Pius IX states that Mary, from the first instant of her conception was freed from original sin and all its effects "in view of the merits of Jesus Christ."[12] This refers to the higher or more sublime manner in which Mary was redeemed, beyond all other children of Adam and Eve. In Mary's redemption, she did not have to suffer the experience of original sin and its effects and later be cleansed through sacramental Baptism, but rather by an application of the foreseen merits of Jesus Christ at Calvary. Preserved from any experience or effect of original sin, she is redeemed in a more sublime manner than the rest of humanity. For this reason, the immaculately conceived mother owes more to her saving Son's redemption than any other redeemed creature.

---

[11] A more technical version of the objection is posed as follows: It appears that Mary cannot participate in the obtaining of the graces of Redemption (commonly deemed objective Redemption) as the Co-Redemptrix when she herself needed to be redeemed. If she did participate as Co-Redemptrix in the obtaining of the graces of Redemption, it is because without her the obtaining of graces has not been accomplished. But if objective Redemption has not been accomplished, then she cannot personally benefit from it.   This would be to accept that objective Redemption is at the same time being accomplished by her, and at the same time has already been accomplished, which would be a contradiction. For extended responses, cf. J. B. Carol, "Our Lady's Coredemption," *Mariology*, vol. 2, (Milwaukee: Bruce Publishing Co., 1957); Friethoff, *A Complete Mariology*, (London: Aquin Press, 1958), 182; J. Galot, S.J., "Maria: Mediatrice o Madre Universale?," *Civilta Cattolica*, 1996, I, pp. 232-244.

[12] Bl. Pius IX, *Ineffabilis Deus*.

How, then, is Mary's redemption enacted so as to allow her to participate in the historic accomplishment of Redemption at Calvary? This higher form of redemption is effected at Calvary in the *first intention of the redemptive sacrifice of Jesus Christ*, which is precisely to redeem Mary.[13] The graces of the first intention are applied to Mary at the moment of her conception, which in turn allows her to become the sinless Co-Redemptrix in union with the universal Redeemer in the Redemption of the rest of the human family — both in intention and accomplishment — at Calvary. There is no contradiction in the historic role of the Co-Redemptrix in the participation of the Redemption and Mary's own personal need and reception of the graces of Redemption. God, who is outside of time, indeed who is the Creator of the temporal order, is not limited by historical necessities, still less is He restrained by our limited understanding of His purposes. He can do as He wills. And in the absolutely unique gift of the Immaculate Conception, He has done so. As Vatican theological consultor, Fr. Jean Galot summarizes:

> The first intention of the redemptive sacrifice was concerned, according to the divine plan, with the ransom of Mary, accomplished in view of our ransom . . . Thus, while she was associated in the sacrifice of Calvary, Mary already benefited, in advance, from the fruits of the sacrifice and acted in the capacity of a ransomed creature. But she truly cooperated in the objective redemption, in the acquisition of the graces of salvation for all of mankind. Her redemption was purchased before that of other human beings. Mary was ransomed only by Christ, so that mankind could be ransomed with the collaboration of his mother ...
>
> Hence there is no contradiction: Marian co-redemption implies the foreseen redemption of Mary, but not the foreseen fulfillment of the redemption of mankind; it expresses the unique situation of the mother who, while having received a singular grace from her own Son, cooperates with Him in the attainment of salvation for all.[14]

---

[13] For an extended treatment, cf. Carol, "Our Lady's Coredemption,"; Friethoff, *A Complete Mariology*, 182; Galot, "Maria: Mediatrice o Madre Universale?," pp. 232-244.

[14] Galot, "Maria Corredentrice: Controversie e problemi dottrinali," *Civilta Cattolica*, 1994, III, p. 218.

Does this primordial intention of Jesus Christ to redeem His mother and then, as subsequent intention, the rest of humanity violate the "one sacrifice" of Jesus Christ offered for all as discussed in Hebrews (cf. Heb. 10:10)? It does not, as the Redemption remains one, although its intentions and efficacious applications are twofold. The one redemptive sacrifice of Jesus Christ at Calvary does not constitute "two redemptions," but one sublime Redemption with two saving applications: the first application effecting the Immaculate Conception of Mary and thus preparing her to be the Co-Redemptrix in her cooperation in objective Redemption; the second application effecting the Redemption of the human family accomplished with the Co-Redemptrix.[15]

We can see then how foundational was the grace of the Immaculate Conception. Indeed, Mary is *"The Co-Redemptrix"* because she was first *"The Immaculate Conception."*

II.   Development and Controversy

The crowning of Our Lady with the dogmatic definition of the Immaculate Conception in 1854 was preceded by a history of intense theological controversy. It was, in fact, one of the fiercest and lengthiest theological debates in the history of Catholic doctrinal development.[16] Much light can be obtained by examining the controversy leading to this Marian dogma, in terms of the process of general doctrinal development (which encompasses the guidance of the Spirit of Truth working through the instrumentality of frail and fallen human

---

[15] Cf. Carol, "Our Lady's Coredemption," p. 418.

[16] For a more comprehensive treatment of the history of the doctrinal development of the Immaculate Conception, cf. G. Roschini, O.S.M., *Maria Sanctissima Nella Storia Della Salvezza*, vol. 3, pp. 37-219; A. Carr, O.F.M.Conv., G. Williams, O.F.M.Conv., "Mary's Immaculate Conception," *Mariology*, vol. 1, (Milwaukee: Bruce Publishing Co., 1955), 344-370; A. Robichaud, S.M., "Immaculate Conception in the Magisterium of the Church," *Marian Studies* 5 (1954). A majority of citations presented here were located from these extended works.

nature), and in evaluating contemporary Mariological doctrinal development, specifically the present discussion concerning the doctrine of Mary Co-Redemptrix.

We can summarize the extensive history of the development of the doctrine of the Immaculate Conception, which spans numerous centuries and hundreds of theologians, by examining the major pronouncements and teachings, as well as censures and penalties, promulgated by the Papal Magisterium in the course of the second Christian millennium. The teachings and disciplines of the Holy See offer an example of the ebb and flow, the agonies and ecstasies relative to the Immaculate Conception doctrine which preceded the *ex cathedra* victory of Bl. Pius IX in 1854, when, guided and protected by the Holy Spirit, he proclaimed it as a Marian dogma.

Founded upon the inspired Word, which implicitly reveals the Mother of the Redeemer as being in "enmity" with sin (Gen. 3:15) and "full of grace" (Lk. 1:28), the Fathers of the Church attributed numerous titles to Our Lady, which bespeaks their gradual awareness of her immunity from original sin and her plenitude of grace. Bl. Pius IX provides examples of this Patristic witness in the defining constitution:

> This doctrine so filled the minds and souls of our ancestors in the faith that a singular and truly marvelous style of speech came into vogue among them. They have frequently addressed the Mother of God as immaculate, as immaculate in every respect; innocent, and verily most innocent; spotless, and entirely spotless; holy and removed from every stain of sin; all pure, all stainless, the very model of purity and innocence; more beautiful than beauty, more lovely than loveliness; more holy than holiness, singularly holy and most pure in soul and body; the one who surpassed all integrity and virginity; the only one who has become the dwelling place of all the graces of the most Holy Spirit. God alone excepted, Mary is more excellent than all, and by nature fair and beautiful, and more holy than the Cherubim and Seraphim. To praise her all the tongues of heaven and earth do not suffice.[17]

---

[17] Bl. Pius IX, *Ineffabilis Deus*.

The Patristic testimonies, particularly from the East, were generous and numerous. In the fourth century, St. Ephraem incorporates the venerated New Eve model in comparing Mary's stainlessness to Eve before Eve's fall: "Those two innocent . . . women, Mary and Eve, had been created utterly equal, but afterwards one became the cause of our death, the other the cause of our life."[18] The Syrian "Harp of the Holy Spirit" then sings of her in an address to Jesus: "Thou and Thy Mother are the only ones immune from all stain; for there is no spot in Thee, O Lord, nor any taint in thy Mother."[19]

From the West, St. Ambrose testifies that the Mother of Jesus was "free from all stain of sin."[20] Severus, bishop of Antioch declares that "She . . . formed part of the human race, and was of the same essence as we, although she was pure from all taint and immaculate."[21] St. Sophronious, the seventh century patriarch of Jerusalem, refers to a pre-purification of grace in the case of Mary: "You have found the grace that no one has received . . . no one has been pre-purified besides you."[22] St. Andrew of Crete calls her the "pure and entirely Immaculate Virgin,"[23] and the ninth century monk, Theognostes of Constantinople directly mentions Our Lady's immaculate origin from conception: " . . . she who from the beginning had been conceived by sanctifying action . . . ."[24]

It is against this background of Tradition's positive laud of the Immaculate Conception during the first Christian millennium, that St. Bernard of Clairvaux writes his historic letter to the Church of Lyons (c.1140), adversely affecting the doctrine's acceptance for the next several centuries. The great Doctor of Marian Mediation, who rightly proclaimed "*de Maria numquam satis*,"[25] nonetheless felt compelled to reject

[18] St. Ephraem, *Sermones exegetici; opere omnia syriace et latine*, 2.
[19] St. Ephraem, *Carmina nisibena*, 27.
[20] St. Ambrose, *Expositio in ps. 118, serm.* 22, n. 30; *PL* 15, 1599.
[21] St. Severus, *Hom. Cathedralis*, 67; *PO* 8, 350.
[22] St. Sophronius, *Orat. in Deiparae Annunt.*, 25; *PG* 87, 3246-3247.
[23] St. Andrew of Crete, *Hom. 1 in nativ. Deiparae*; *PG* 97, 813-814.
[24] Theognostes, *Hom. in dormit. Deiparae*; *PO* 16, 457.
[25] "Of Mary, never enough."

this prerogative of his Queen due to a mistaken notion of the transmission of original sin.

In his letter to the canons of Lyons who had begun to celebrate the Feast of the Conception of Mary, St. Bernard rejects the feast and the doctrine behind it on the basis of the Augustinian notion that conception was directly connected with concupiscence. According to St. Augustine,[26] original sin infected the human body, which then automatically infected the soul at its infusion into the body. Mary, therefore, could not have been sanctified at her conception, but only in the womb after conception, and this act "rendered her birth holy, not her conception."[27]

Almost two centuries later, the Church is gifted with the theological breakthrough of the Subtle Doctor, Bl. John Duns Scotus (†1308) and the proper understanding that original sin is not passed on through infected body to infected soul upon the soul's creation and infusion, but rather through a privation of grace in the soul at the moment of conception due to the sin of Adam and Eve.[28] The rejection of the doctrine by St. Bernard, St. Thomas Aquinas,[29] St. Albert the Great,[30] St. Bonaventure,[31] and other scholastics, many of whom are significantly influenced by St. Bernard, is the dominant historical setting during the early part of the second millennium, a situation which eventually calls for the intervention of the Papal Magisterium.

The Feast of the Conception of Mary continues to spread, in spite of the theological opposition, to become an almost general celebration in the West. By the mid-fourteenth century, the feast is solemnly celebrated in Rome,[32] and later

---

[26] Cf. St. Augustine, *Contra Julianum*, ch. 15, n. 54; *PL* 44, 814.

[27] St. Bernard of Clairvaux, *Epist. 174, ad canonicos lugdunenses*; *PL* 182, 332-336.

[28] Bl. John Duns Scotus, *Opus Oxoniense*, lib. 3, dist. 3, p. 1.

[29] St. Thomas Aquinas, *In 3 Sent.*, dist. 3, p. 1, art. 2; id., *Summa Theologica*, III, 27, 2, ad. 2.

[30] St. Albert the Great, *In 3 Sent.*, dist. 3, art. 5.

[31] St. Bonaventure, *In 3 Sent.*, dist. 3, pars 1, art. 1, q. 2.

[32] J. B. Malou, *L'Immaculée Conception de la bienheureuse Vierge Marie*

in the century by the "Sovereign Pontiff and by the Cardinals" in unison.[33] It must be kept in mind that the nature of the feast at this time constituted a celebration of the general sanctification of Mary in the womb of St. Ann, without the clear delineation of the exact nature and time of the actual sanctification.

At about the same time, Pope Gregory XI approves the well-known *Revelations* of St. Bridget of Sweden, with his two immediate papal successors, Urban VI and Boniface IX, confirming the approbation.[34] The Revelations record Our Lady's words that: "It is the truth that I was conceived without original sin,"[35] and explains further:

> Believe, my daughter, seeing that they think rightly who believe and profess that I was preserved from the original stain; wrongly, however, those who think the contrary, especially if they do so with temerity.[36]

> . . . Know that I was conceived without original sin, and not in sin. . . Know that my Conception was not known to all because God willed it that way . . . thus it was pleasing to God that his friends would piously doubt of my Conception, and each would manifest his zeal, until the truth would be clarified at its foreordained time.[37]

considérée comme dogme de foi, vol. 1, Brussels, 1857, p. 131; Cherubinus Sericoli, O.F.M., *Immaculata B.M. Virginis Conceptio iuxta Xysti IV Constitutiones*, Rome 1945, pp. 12-13; cf. Robichaud, "Immaculate Conception," p. 88.

[33] P. Doncoeur, S.J., "Les premières interventions du St. Siège relatives à l'Immaculée Conception, XII-XIV siècles," *Revue d'histoire ecclésiastique*, vol. 8, 1907, p. 700; Le Bachelet, S.J., "Immaculée Conception," *Dictionnaire de Théologie Catholique*, Paris, 1903, vol. 7, col. 1101; cf. Robichaud, "Immaculate Conception," p. 90.

[34] Cf. Pourrat, "Brigitte," *Catholicisme*, Paris, vol. 2, 1949, col. 271-272; cf. Robichaud, "Immaculate Conception," p. 92.

[35] St. Bridget of Sweden, *Revelations*, bk. 6, ch. 49.

[36] *Ibid.*

[37] St. Bridget, *Revelations*, bk. 6, ch. 55; cf. D. Cerri., "Enchiridion auctoritatum super duodecim . . . triumphos B. Mariae Virginis Matris Dei in originale peccatum," *Pareri dell'Episcopato Cattolico . . . sulla definizione dogmatica dell'Immacolato Concepimento della Beata Virgine Maria*, Rome, 1852, part 3, vol. 6, 1852, p. 174; cf. Robichaud, "Immaculate Conception," p. 92.

As the *Revelations* were widely promulgated and respected throughout medieval Christendom, its influence was significant upon theologians and bishops alike in growth of support for the Immaculate Conception. We see here one example of the direct influence of authentic private revelation in the historical development of doctrine, not as a legitimate foundation for the doctrine, but rather as a supernatural spark to stimulate development at an appropriate historical time in the Church's life and thought.

The Council of Basle which convenes in the mid-fifteenth century (Sept. 17, 1439) attempts to define the Immaculate Conception doctrine in their declaration from the 37th session, which states:

> . . . We define and declare that the doctrine according to which the glorious Virgin Mary, Mother of God, by a special effect of divine preventing and operating grace, was never stained with original sin, but has always been holy and immaculate, is a pious doctrine, conformable to the cult of the Church, to Catholic Faith, to right reason, and Sacred Scripture; it must be approved, held and professed by all Catholics; furthermore, it is no longer allowed to preach or teach anything contrary to it.[38]

Even though the Council had been placed under an anathema by Pope Eugene IV (due to its papal stance, something not immediately relevant to the issue of the Immaculate Conception), the declaration nevertheless illustrates the depth of theological and hierarchical commitment to the doctrine at this time.

But new attacks on the doctrine are soon to surface in the latter part of the fifteenth century. History bears out the fact that *Marian dogmatic development is typically juxtaposed with fierce and repeated theological conflict, and oftentimes between bishops and theologians in full fidelity to the Holy See.*

---

[38] Le Bachelet, "Immaculée Conception," col. 1113; Sericoli, *Immaculata B.M. Virginis*, p. 21; Malou, *L'Immaculée Conception*, p. 60; cf. Robichaud, "Immaculate Conception," p. 94.

III.   Sixtus IV and Papal Approval of the Feast

The Franciscan Pope, Sixtus IV (1471-1484) is the first pontiff to make an official magisterial pronouncement relative to the Immaculate Conception. Pope Sixtus issues sixteen constitutions with reference to Mary's Conception,[39] but the first major bull is issued in 1477 and entitled, *Cum praecelsa*. In this Bull, the pontiff officially approves the prayers of the Office of the Conception, and grants indulgences for those who recite the Office or attend Mass in its honor.[40]

The atmosphere at the time the bull is promulgated involves an intense theological battle over the issue, essentially between the Dominican and the Franciscan orders. Dominican theologian Vincent Bandelli had written a book two years prior in which he strongly attacked the Immaculate Conception doctrine as impious, heretical, contrary to the teaching of the Church, and to sound reason.[41] This leads Sixtus IV to order a public disputation on the issue in his presence in Rome in early 1477. Fr. Bandelli defends his Maculist position, and the Minister General of the Franciscans, Francis Insuber of Brescia articulates the Immaculist stance. The Immaculist position proves victorious, which leads Sixtus IV to immediately grant official approval to the Mass and Office of the Conception of Mary.[42]

The papally approved feast is clearly and specifically Immaculist, with Our Lady being referred to as "Immaculate" ten times, and with some thirty references to her having been conceived without original sin,[43] using phrases such as:

---

[39] Sericoli, *Immaculata B.M. Virginis*, pp. 26, 29.

[40] J. D. Mansi, *Sacrorum Conciliorum Nova et Amplissima Collectio*, 32, Paris-Leipzig, 1901, 373-374. For information on Sixtus IV, cf. Sericoli, *ibid*.

[41] V. Bandelli, *Libellus recolectorius auctoritatum de veritate conceptionis B.V. Mariae*, Milan, 1475.

[42] Sericoli, *Immaculata B.M. Virginis*, pp. 31-33.

[43] Sericoli, *ibid.*, p. 80.

> You are all beautiful, O Mary, and the stain of original sin is not in thee [2nd antiphon of 1st Vesp.].[44]

And:

> Today is the Immaculate Conception of the Holy Virgin Mary. God who, by the Immaculate Conception of the Virgin, did prepare a worthy dwelling . . . grant, we beseech thee, who by his foreseen death did preserve her from all stain of sin . . . [Collect of the Mass and Oration of the Office].[45]

But the papal sanction does not end the controversy. Bandelli authors another book in 1481, in which he seeks to interpret the Pope's document as referring to Mary's sanctification after the instance of animation, thus inferring that it teaches her "spiritual conception" and not her natural immaculate conception. Moreover, opponents do not celebrate the papally approved feast, but rather return to the more generic feast of "Mary's Sanctification."[46]

This leads Sixtus IV to respond with the bull *Grave nimis* in 1482, in which he threatens to excommunicate the objectors and also those who charge their opponents with heresy. He also condemns any who claim that the Holy See was referring only to the spiritual conception of Mary or the general sanctification of Mary. But, in the second issue of the bull, *Grave nimis* (posterior) in 1484, the Pontiff also forbids the Immaculists to accuse their opponents of being guilty of the "crime of heresy or of mortal sin, since the matter has not been decided as yet by the Roman Church and the Apostolic See."[47] Because the Church has not yet formally decided the doctrinal question, proponents and opponents of the feast alike cannot be declared heretical or in grave sin *per se*.[48]

Considering the clarity and firmness of Sixtus IV's intervention, one can imagine that the "pious belief" of the Immaculate Conception (as it was termed) would be essen-

[44] Sericoli, *ibid.*; cf. Robichaud, "Immaculate Conception," p. 98.
[45] *Ibid.*
[46] Mansi, *Sacrorum Conciliorum*, 374-375.
[47] Sericoli, *Immaculata B.M. Virginis*, appendix.
[48] *Ibid.*

tially free from any accusation of heresy, and that doctrinal development leading to the definition in 1854 would proceed in a fundamentally peaceful process. Moreover, in a promising move, Sixtus' successor, Innocent VIII, immediately follows his predecessor's initiatives by approving a religious congregation from Spain with the title, "Religious of the Immaculate Conception of Mary" in the Bull, *Inter innumera* (1489).[49] However, *the next three centuries would witness ubiquitous theological standoffs, strong papal interventions, and serious ecclesiastical censures, all of which would constitute the tumultuous journey of this doctrine to the nineteenth century solemn definition.*

The Council of Trent in the sixteenth century sought in general to restrict its doctrinal treatments to the specific areas brought into question by Protestant objections. Nonetheless, when the subject of the universality of original sin is brought up during the fifth session in 1546, the issue is raised as to whether or not the Mother of Jesus was subject to the universal law. Immediately, a number of theological debates ensue. After much intense discussion, the Council concludes with the following declaration:

> This same holy Synod declares that it is not its intention to include in this decree, where there is question of original sin, the blessed and immaculate Virgin Mary, Mother of God. Rather, the constitutions of Sixtus of happy memory are to be followed.[50]

Trent, therefore, refers to the Mother of Jesus as "Immaculate"; does not include her within the universal law of original sin; and refers to Pope Sixtus and his defense of the Immaculist position. As Bl. Pius IX comments in *Ineffabilis Deus*, the Council of Trent "sufficiently insinuat-

---

[49] Malou, *L'Immaculée Conception*, pp. 148, 156; C. Passaglia, S.J., *De Immaculato Deiparae semper Virginis conceptu*, Rome, 1855, vol. 3, pp. 1782-1783; Letter of the Bishop of Málaga, Spain, *Pareri*, part 1, vol. 3, p. 12; Letter of the Bishop of Toledo, Spain, *Pareri*, part 1, vol. 3, p. 121; Cerri, "Enchiridion," pp. 111, 112.

[50] Concilium Trident, sess. 5; *DB* 792.

ed by this declaration that the Blessed Virgin Mary was free from the original stain."[51]

And yet controversy continues. In 1567, the great Marian pontiff, St. Pius V condemns one of the propositions of Baius, which reads: "No one but Christ was without original sin, and therefore the Blessed Virgin died in consequence of the sin contracted through Adam . . . ."[52] The Dominican pontiff also issues a bull, *Super speculam*, in 1570, in which he speaks of the evil effects of the controversy which continues to rage over the Immaculate Conception. In an effort to prevent the present scandal from infecting the faithful, St. Pius V renews the teachings and censures of Sixtus IV, the Council of Trent, and adds the following new restrictions: ". . . no one is allowed to discuss either of the opinions in sermons given before the people . . . or to write or dictate anything in the vernacular on the question."[53]

Note the paternal character of Pius V's actions. He acts as a good father of the family who enters into a heated family conflict, and intervenes by first reiterating the truth and then by calling a halt to any further discussion until emotions settle. The specific concern of Pius was the scandal being caused amidst the common faithful. We will repeatedly see the importance of the *sensus fidelium* in this historical drama.

Despite this, the theological battle rages on, and seventeenth century popes once again come to the defense of the doctrine. In 1616, Pope Paul V issues the Bull, *Regis pacifici*, in which he recalls the pronouncement of Sixtus IV, Trent, and Pius V, but notes that these did not suffice to stop the conflict. Paul V therefore reiterates with "Apostolic power" his predecessors' teachings, but with additional punishments for offenders.[54] A year later, the ecclesial storm still continues, and Paul V

---

[51] Bl. Pius IX, *Ineffabilis Deus*.
[52] *Bullarium Privilegiorum ac Diplomatum Romanorum Pontificium*, vol. 4, part 3, p. 429; *DB* 1073.
[53] St. Pius V, Bull *Super speculam*, 1570; *Bullarium Romanorum, ibid.*, p. 138.
[54] *Bullarium Romanorum*, vol. 5, part 4, pp. 209-211.

issues a decree, *Sanctissimus* (Sept. 12, 1617) whereby the Roman pontiff for the first time officially forbids anyone from denying the Immaculate Conception in public.[55] The expressed reason for the papal action is the scandal, quarrels, and dissensions caused among the common faithful whenever public sermons or teachings deny the Immaculate Conception or positively teach that she was conceived with original sin. In short, the denial of the Immaculate Conception is rejected by the *sensus fidelium*, and the Vicar of Christ respects and protects the Spirit acting through them.[56]

A few years later, Pope Gregory XV extends the prohibitions of Paul V against the public denial of the Immaculate Conception to the realm of private conversations and writings as well, until such time as the Holy See would resolve the issue.[57] Once again, this papal directive requiring absolute silence for those denying the Immaculate Conception is prompted by the reaction of the common consensus of the faithful.[58] It is also noteworthy at this time that heads of state begin requesting the Holy See for a papal definition of the Immaculate Conception, with repeated petitions coming from the Kings of Spain.[59]

---

[55] Paul V, Decree *Sanctissimus*, September 12, 1617; *Bullarium Romanorum*, *ibid.*, pp. 234-235.

[56] Cf. Robichaud, "Immaculate Conception," p. 113.

[57] Gregory XV, Decree *Sanctissimus*, June 2, 1622: "Hoc suo praesente decreto. . . extendit et ampliavit etiam ad privata colloquia et scripta, mandans et praecipiens omnibus et singulis supradictis, ne de cetero. . . neque etiam in sermonibus et scriptis privates audeant asserere, quod eadem Beatissima Virgo fuerit concepta cum peccato originali, nec de hac opinione affirmativa aliquo modo agree, seu tractare, exceptis tamen quibus a Sancta Sede Apostolica fuerit super hoc specialiter indultum." Cf. *Bullarium Romanorum*, vol. 5, part 5, p. 45.

[58] *Ibid.* Note: Special exception was made for the private discussion of the issue among the Dominicans in a decree issued one month after *Sanctissimus*. Cf. *Bullarium Romanorum*, *ibid.*, p. 46.

[59] For example, in 1627 Pope Urban VIII received a formal request from Philip IV of Spain for its definition; cf. P. Guéranger, "Mémoire sur la question de l'Immaculée Conception . . ." *Pareri*, part 3, vol. 7, p. 28; Le Bachelet, "Immaculée Conception," col. 1174; J. Mansella, *Il Domma*

Under the pontificate of Urban VIII, a pontiff who also advances the cause of the Immaculate Conception through the granting of generous indulgences relative to the doctrine,[60] we have an interesting historical case of a decree contrary to the doctrine being drawn up by the Holy Office a few months before Urban's death and published three years after his death. The decree from the Holy Office states: "It is not permitted to attribute the title of 'Immaculate' to the Conception of the Blessed Virgin; one must say the Conception of the Immaculate Mary."[61] It is generally agreed upon by historians that the Holy Office decree did not have the approval of the Holy Father.[62] We see here an instance of how a doctrinal Congregation can err on a disciplinary matter relative to a doctrine when it does not have direct pontifical approval.

With the papal election of Alexander VII in 1661, the doctrine gains one of its greatest papal champions. In the Bull, *Sollicitudo omnium Ecclesiarum*, Alexander exacts the nature of the feast of the Immaculate Conception as the belief of Mary's immunity from original sin at conception, refers to the doctrine as a "*pia sententia*," or "pious belief," (a theological category of certainty that had been proposed but not approved at Trent[63]), and confirms and broadens the canonical penalties of his papal predecessors for those rejecting the doctrine.[64]

In 1708, Pope Clement XI provides further magisterial foundation for an eventual definition in the Bull, *Commissi*

---

dell'Immacolata Concezione della Beata Virgine Maria, Rome, 1866, vol. 1, p. 218.

[60] Cf. Urban VIII, *Cum sicut accepimus*, 1639.

[61] Archangelus a Roc, O.F.M.Cap., "Joannes Maria Zamoro ab Udine, O.F.M.Cap., praeclarus mariologus," *Collectanea Franciscana*, Rome, 1945-1949, vols. 15-19, p. 117; Le Bachelet, "Immaculée Conception," col. 1174; cf. Robichaud, "Immaculate Conception," p. 118.

[62] *Ibid.*

[63] Cf. Robichaud, "Immaculate Conception," p. 120.

[64] Cf. *Bullarium Romanorum*, vol. 6, part 5, pp. 182-184.

Nobis, by establishing the feast of the Immaculate Conception as a holy day of obligation for the entire Catholic Church.[65] Little more than a century later, Pope Gregory XVI, the immediate predecessor of Bl. Pius IX, grants permission for an additional petition to the Litany of Loreto to read: "Queen conceived without original sin, pray for us."[66]

By the nineteenth century, the Holy See has received and continues to receive numerous petitions for the solemn definition, both from the hierarchy and from the common faithful.[67] So significant is the factor of petitions from the People of God to the pontiff in the development of this Marian doctrine that Bl. Pius IX refers to the positive role of petitions as one of the legitimate criterion for its solemn definition in *Ineffabilis Deus*.[68] Far from the mistaken notion that petitions directed to Rome are merely a contemporary invention for democratized pressure within the Church, petitions from the hierarchy and the common faithful comprise a substantial element in the true papal discernment for solemn definitions.[69]

Another positive influence for Bl. Pius IX in his discernment for the infallible declaration is the Church-approved apparitions of Our Lady of Grace received by St. Catherine Labouré in 1830, in which the "Medal of the Immaculate Conception" is revealed by Our Lady and swiftly spreads throughout Europe and beyond. The petition surrounding the "Miraculous Medal," as it was spontaneously referred to by the faithful, reads "O Mary conceived without sin, pray for us who have recourse to thee." The immediate and universal acceptance of this medal so essentially linked to the Immaculate

---

[65] *Ibid.*, vol. 11, part 1, p. 206.

[66] J. Bourassé, *Summa aurea de laudibus B.M.V.*, Paris, 1862, vol. 7, col. 608-612; *Pareri*, part 3, vol. 6, pp. 574-579.

[67] Cf. Bl. Pius IX, *Ineffabilis Deus*; Malou, *L'Immaculée Conception*, p. 216

[68] Cf. Bl. Pius IX, *Ineffabilis Deus*, middle section of the document.

[69] This is confirmed by both Bl. Pius IX and Pius XII in relation to their respective Marian *ex cathedra* definitions. Cf. Bl. Pius IX, *Ineffabilis Deus*; Pius XII, Apostolic Constitution of the Solemn Definition of the Assumption, *Munificentissimus Deus*, November 1, 1950; *AAS* 42, 1950, p. 754.

Conception doctrine and the plethora of miracles associated with it, make a strong positive impression on Pius IX.[70]

In summation, centuries of fierce theological battles moderated by papal interventions, juxtaposed with a persevering liturgical, theological, and devotional development, serve as the historical platform upon which Bl. Pius IX courageously crowns the Virgin Mother of God with the dogmatic definition of the Immaculate Conception on December 8, 1854. The historical tempest which precedes the definition seems to symbolically manifest itself on the actual day of the definition by a violent storm outside of St. Peter's Basilica. As Sardi, the respected documenter of the history and acts concerning the definition, then describes:

> At the precise moment His Holiness was going to define the dogma, a light breeze lifted the drape in front of the great window above the altar of the Chapel of Most Holy Mary of the Pillar, and a sunbeam lit up the person of the Holy Father and his pontifical throne. Many marveled at this event because of the solemn moment when it occurred . . . .[71]

IV.   Immaculate Conception and Mary Co-Redemptrix: Parallels in Doctrinal Development

The Holy Spirit guides and nurtures a seed of revelation found in the Word of God, written or handed down, so that it takes root and grows gradually to full blossom and beauty within the garden of the Church in the form of a defined dogma. As the Spirit is one, so are His ways similar and detectable within the process of this development of doctrine. While there is always some dimension of the beauty of diversity within the movements of the Spirit, so too is there a certain uniformity and pattern.

---

[70] J. Dirvin, C.M., *St. Catherine Labouré of the Miraculous Medal*, (Rockford: Tan, 1958), 178; cf. R. Laurentin, *Catherine Labouré et la Médaille Miraculeuse*, Paris, 1976.

[71] V. Sardi, *La solenne definizione del dogma dell'Immacolato Concepimento di Maria SS., Atti e documenti*, vol. 2, p. 428.

In this light, we find at least seven similarities, true parallels of doctrinal maturation, as we juxtapose the development of the Immaculate Conception with that of Mary Co-Redemptrix. In the case of the Immaculate Conception doctrine, these stages or levels of maturity eventually led to its solemn definition. So, too, the presence of *these same seven characteristics* in the development of the Co-Redemptrix doctrine offers significant evidence for its own doctrinal maturity.

1. Longstanding Liturgical Feast of Our Lady of Sorrows

Of great significance is the papal approval of the Feast of The Conception of Mary by Sixtus IV in 1477 and its critical role in the Immaculate Conception's doctrinal progression. In the case of Mary Co-Redemptrix, we also have a liturgical feast celebrated in Rome which likewise dates back to the fifteenth century, the Feast of Our Lady of Sorrows.

In fact, until 1960, the role of Mary Co-Redemptrix was liturgically celebrated twice a year. The first feast focused upon the "compassion" or co-suffering of Mary at Calvary and was celebrated on the Friday before our present Palm Sunday. The second feast, historically promoted by the Servites of Mary and celebrated on September 15, accentuates the entire coredemptive life of the Virgin as highlighted in seven scriptural and traditional events or "sorrows": 1. Simeon's prophecy in the Temple; 2. the flight of the Holy Family into Egypt; 3. the loss of the Christ Child in the Temple; 4. the encounter of Mary with Jesus on the way of the cross; 5. her suffering during the crucifixion and death of Jesus; 6. the taking down of Jesus from the Cross; and 7. the burial of Jesus in the tomb.

Moreover, the first official use of the Co-Redemptrix title by the Holy See comes on May 13, 1908, in a document by the Congregation of Rites in reference to the Feast of the

Seven Sorrows. In positive response to a petition seeking to raise the rank of the feast of the Seven Sorrows of Mary to a double rite of second class for the universal Church, the Congregation of Rites expresses its hope that "the devotion of the Sorrowful Mother may increase and the piety of the faithful and their gratitude toward the merciful Co-Redemptrix of the human race may intensify."[72]

These liturgical celebrations of the Co-Redemptrix doctrine makes clear that the role has been believed and venerated for over a half millennium in the liturgical life of the Church.

2. Conciliar Teaching on Marian Coredemption

The conciliar teaching of Trent on the Immaculate Conception doctrine, however implicit, nonetheless clearly established the doctrinal integrity of the position. In addition, there were those at Trent who desired a solemn definition of the Immaculate Conception,[73] but the Council saw it sufficient for that time to reflect the legitimacy of the doctrine in its other teachings.

The Second Vatican Council in its preparatory stage similarly received over 450 petitions for the solemn definition of the Mary Co-Redemptrix and her subsequent role as Mediatrix of all graces[74] and deemed it sufficient for the purposes of a non-defining pastoral council to present a certain teaching on Marian Coredemption. The Council did so in its Dogmatic Constitution on the Church, *Lumen Gentium*. In the eighth chapter, which is dedicated to Our Lady, the Fathers clearly teach her coredemptive role:

---

[72] *AAS* 1, 1908, p. 409.
[73] Cf. Carol, *Fundamentals of Mariology*, (New York: Benzinger Bros., 1956), 107.
[74] Cf. G. M. Besutti, O.S.M., *Lo Schema Mariano al Concilio Vaticano II*, Edizioni Marianum, 1966, p. 17; cf. M. Miravalle, *"With Jesus": The Story of Mary Co-redemptrix*, (Santa Barbara: Queenship, 2003), 167.

Committing herself whole-heartedly and impeded by no sin to God's saving will, she devoted herself totally, as a handmaid of the Lord, to the person and work of her Son, under and with him, serving the mystery of redemption . . . (LG, 56).

And:

Thus the Blessed Virgin advanced in her pilgrimage of faith, and faithfully persevered in her union with her Son unto the cross, where she stood, in keeping with the divine plan, enduring with her only begotten Son the intensity of his suffering, associated herself with his sacrifice in her mother's heart, and lovingly consenting to the immolation of this victim which was born of her. Finally, she was given by the same Christ Jesus dying on the cross as a mother to his disciple, with these words: "Woman, behold thy son" (Jn. 19:26-27) (LG, 58).

And further:

She conceived, brought forth, and nourished Christ, she presented him to the Father in the temple, shared her Son's sufferings as he died on the cross. Thus, in a wholly singular way she cooperated by her obedience, faith, hope and burning charity in the work of the Savior in restoring supernatural life to souls. For this reason she is a mother to us in the order of grace (LG, 61).

The fact that the Second Vatican Council, which was pastoral by nature (as determined at its outset by Bl. John XXIII), did not define the Coredemption doctrine cannot be used as a valid argument against its definability. Trent did not define the Immaculate Conception, nor did Vatican I define the Assumption, although it had received from participating Fathers numerous petitions to do so.[75] Rather, the solid conciliar teaching on the truth of the Co-Redemptrix role reflects an unquestionable theological basis in the sources of Revelation for a potential definition.

---

[75] Cf. Pius XII, *Munificentissimus Deus*, p. 754-755.

3. Petitions from the Faithful, Hierarchy, and Heads of State

Bl. Pius IX's acknowledgement of the numerous petitions from the hierarchy, common faithful, and even heads of states received by the Holy See for the Immaculate Conception's definition illustrates the papal respect given to the *sensus fidelium* in the process of discerning the timeliness and appropriateness of infallible declarations. Pius XII made the same acknowledgement for the vast number of petitions received in favor of the Dogma of the Assumption.[76]

The largest number of per annum petitions received by the Holy See for any single cause in the history of the Church has been for the solemn definition of Mary Co-Redemptrix. In the last ten years, over seven million petitions have been received by the Holy See from over one hundred and fifty countries in support of this infallible declaration.[77] More than five hundred and fifty bishops, including forty six cardinals, have also joined in the petition during the past ten years.[78]

As Spain was foremost in national support for the Dogma of the Immaculate Conception, the Philippines and Mexico are leaders in the national calls for the definition of Mary Co-Redemptrix. Over seventy percent of the Mexican hierarchy has petitioned the Holy Father for the definition.[79] The Philippines have produced the largest number of lay petitions. Former Philippines President, Mrs. Corazon Aquino, petitioned the Holy See for the dogmatic proclamation while in office.

4. Indulgenced Prayers in Relation to Mary Co-Redemptrix

Lex orandi, lex credendi — as the Church prays, so she believes. The indulgences approved by the Holy See for

---

[76] Cf. *Ibid.*

[77] *Vox Populi Mariae Mediatrici* petition center archives, PO Box 220, Goleta, CA 93116, May, 2003.

[78] Note: These numbers reflect only the last ten years, without including the great number of hierarchical petitions for the dogma prior to 1993; cf. *Vox Populi* petition archives.

[79] Cf. *Vox Populi* petition archives.

prayers associated with the Immaculate Conception also finds its parallel with the Co-Redemptrix doctrine.

On June 26, 1913, the Holy Office issued a document expressing the Congregation's satisfaction in adding the name of Mary to the name of Jesus in the indulgenced greeting, "*Praised* be Jesus and Mary" which is then responded to, "Now and forever." The document then states: "There are those Christians whose devotion to the most favored among virgins is so tender as to be unable to recall the name of Jesus without the accompanying name of the Mother, our Co-redemptrix, the Blessed Virgin Mary."[80]

Six months later, the same Holy Office granted a partial indulgence for the recitation of a prayer of reparation to the Blessed Virgin (*Vergine benedetta*). The prayer ends with the words: "I bless thy holy Name, I praise thine exalted privilege of being truly Mother of God, ever Virgin, conceived without stain of sin, Co-redemptrix of the human race."[81]

5. Religious Congregations Bearing the Co-Redemptrix Name

As was the case with Innocent VIII and the approval of the "Religious of the Immaculate Conception of Mary," congregations with the Co-Redemptrix title have received Church approval. The North Vietnamese religious congregation, "The Congregation of the Mother Co-redemptrix," which was approved by the local bishop in 1941 and approved by the Holy See in 1953, was forced to relocate to South Vietnam due to Communist persecution, and later expanded to the United States.[82] Presently, a religious congregation of priests and religious found in Italy, Slovakia, Russia, the Netherlands, and several other countries, with

---

[80] *AAS* 5, 1913, p. 364.
[81] *AAS* 6, 1914, p. 108.
[82] Cf. *The Official Catholic Directory*, P. J. Kenedy and Sons, 2003, p. 1305.

the name of "The Family of Mary Co-redemptrix" is rapidly growing in vocations, particularly in Eastern Europe.

6. Private Revelation Stimulating and Confirming the Co-Redemptrix Doctrine

As the *Revelations* of St. Bridget and the apparitions of the Miraculous Medal to St. Catherine Labouré offer stimulation and growth to the Immaculate Conception doctrine, confirmed in the life of the Church, so too has ecclesiastically approved private revelation served to confirm the truth of Mary Co-Redemptrix and, specifically, its eventual solemn definition.

From the same *Revelations* given to St. Bridget of Sweden, Our Lady offers a direct testimony to her role as Co-Redemptrix: "My Son and I redeemed the world as with one heart."[83] Our Lord re-iterates the same truth of the Co-Redemptrix doctrine in His own words: "My Mother and I saved man as with one Heart only, I by suffering in my Heart and my Flesh, She by the sorrow and love of Her Heart."[84] These revelations positively influenced theologians and popes alike for the next three hundred years and were repeatedly referenced by theologians and bishops during the seventeenth century "Golden Age" of Marian Coredemption.[85]

More recently, a number of contemporary Marian apparitions approved by the Church have spoken of the Co-Redemptrix role. The apparitions of Our Lady of Akita in Japan (1973), manifest Our Lady's ongoing coredemptive role in the form of messages and scientifically verified lacrimations.[86] The

---

[83] St. Bridget, *Revelations*, bk. 1, ch. 35.

[84] St. Bridget, *Revelations*, bk. 9, ch. 3.

[85] Cf. Miravalle, *"With Jesus,"* pp. 113-124.

[86] Cf. T. Yasuda, S.V.D., "The Message of Mary Coredemptrix at Akita and Its Complementarity with the Dogma Movement," *Contemporary Insights on a Fifth Marian Dogma, Mary Coredemptrix, Mediatrix, Advocate: Theological Foundations III*, (Santa Barbara: Queenship, 2000), 235-249; F. Fukushima, *Akita: Mother of God as Coredemptrix, Modern Miracles of Holy Eucharist*, (Santa Barbara: Queenship, 1997).

apparitions received ecclesiastical approbation from the local ordinary, Bishop John Ito (1984). The related apparitions of the Lady of All Nations in Amsterdam (1945-1959), which has been declared of supernatural origin by Bishop Josef Punt of Haarlem-Amsterdam (May 31, 2002), contains numerous messages from Our Lady which speak of the roles of Co-Redemptrix, Mediatrix, Advocate, and the eventual solemn definition of these roles. For example, in the message of April 29, 1951:

> I stand here as the Co-Redemptrix and Advocate. Everything should be concentrated on that. Repeat this after me; The new Dogma will be the "dogma of the Co-Redemptrix." Notice I lay special emphasis on "Co." I have said that it will arouse much controversy. Once again I tell you that the Church, "Rome," will carry it through and silence all objections. The Church, "Rome," will incur opposition and overcome it. The Church "Rome," will become stronger and mightier in proportion to the resistance she puts up in the struggle. My purpose and my commission to you is none other than to urge the Church, the theologians, to wage this battle. For the Father, the Son and the Holy Spirit wills to send the Lady, chosen to bear the Redeemer, into this world, as Co-Redemptrix and Advocate.
>
> . . . In the sufferings, both spiritual and bodily, the Lady, the Mother has shared. She has always gone before. As soon as the Father had elected her, she was the Co-Redemptrix with the Redeemer, who came into the world as the Man-God. Tell that to your theologians. I know well, the struggle will be hard and bitter (and then the Lady smiles to herself and seems to gaze into the far distance), but the outcome is already assured.[87]

To be sure, private revelation, even that which is approved by the Church, can never serve as the theological foundation for a Church doctrine or its potential definition. Nevertheless, the history of dogmatic development bears out the fact that "certain supernatural lights which it pleases God to distribute to certain privileged souls," to use the words of Bl. John XXIII,[88] have sparked and assisted the development of certain doctrines at key historical periods of the Church.

---

[87] *The Messages of the Lady of All Nations*, (Santa Barbara: Queenship, 1996), April 29, 1951 message, pp. 49-51.

[88] Bl. John XXIII, Close of the Marian Year, Feb. 18, 1959.

Perhaps our best contemporary example is the new ecclesial emphasis on Divine Mercy, which has been directly stimulated through the revelations to St. Faustina Kowalska, and has inspired the Church to the liturgical development of a universal feast of Divine Mercy on the Sunday following Easter Sunday, as well as the doctrinal development on Divine Mercy for our present troubled age as manifested in the 1982 papal encyclical, *Dives in Misericordia.*

7. Theological Controversy and Mary Co-Redemptrix

If history tells us anything about the journey of Marian dogmas, it is that theological controversy and emotionally charged debate will be their constant companions. This is visible in a dramatic way in the seven centuries of battle over the Immaculate Conception, with some of history's greatest theologians, such as St. Bernard, St. Thomas Aquinas, St. Albert the Great, and St. Bonaventure, finding themselves on the opposing side of the eventual dogma. This is also evident in the prior dogmatic proclamation of Mary as the "God-bearer" at Ephesus (431), with the historic confrontations between St. Cyril of Alexandria, Nestorius, and their respective followers.

Theological controversy in itself, therefore, should never be used as a legitimate argument for the inappropriateness of a doctrine or its definition, as oftentimes the controversy becomes the very reason why the Bishop of Rome is called to speak definitively and bring peace to the family of the Church upon the necessary foundation of the truth.

The fact that the Papal Magisterium has never deemed it necessary to call for a public prohibition of the discussion of Mary Co-Redemptrix due to controversy and its subsequent scandal for the faithful,[89] let alone prohibiting even private discussion as it did for the Immaculate Conception debate,[90]

---

[89] St. Pius V, *Super speculam*; cf. *Bullarium Romanorum*, vol. 4, part 3, p. 138.
[90] Gregory XV, *Sanctissimus*; cf. *Bullarium Romanorum*, vol. 5, part 5, p. 45.

should give a better historical context in which to understand the arguably lesser degree of theological disagreement over Marian Coredemption. This, of course, is due in our own time to the authoritative presentation of the doctrine by the twentieth and twenty-first century Papal Magisterium and the Second Vatican Council.[91]

In light of the clear Church teaching on the doctrine, the hub of debate in the case of Mary Co-Redemptrix focuses more upon the question of its potential definition as a dogma of the Faith. This would historically parallel where the Immaculate Conception development was in the first half of the nineteenth century. Now, as then, the Magisterium has settled the question of doctrinal integrity, and the theological discussion is centered around questions of the appropriateness and timeliness of a solemn definition.[92]

What makes a Marian doctrine definable? It is the establishing of its foundation in divine revelation and its organic maturity in that faith, worship, and life dimension of the Church which we call "Tradition."[93] Both Magisterial and conciliar teachings confirm the foundations of Mary Co-Redemptrix in the sources of Revelation. Certainly the other criteria which, at the time, had indicated doctrinal maturity for the Immaculate Conception are likewise present for the doctrine of Mary Co-Redemptrix (i.e., the liturgical celebration of the role, the unprecedented petitions from the *sensus fidelium* and hierarchy, the private revelational confirmation, etc.), and do in fact offer evidence for its maturity within the Church's contemporary living Tradition.

---

[91] Cf. Miravalle, *"With Jesus,"* chs. 11-13, pp. 149-208.

[92] Note: Although a lack of knowledge of contemporary papal and conciliar teachings on Marian Coredemption has caused unnecessary debate as to even its doctrinal legitimacy.

[93] Cf. Second Vatican Council, *Dei Verbum*, November 18, 1965, ch. 2.

Conclusion

May the Holy Spirit, through the Immaculate Conception, enlighten the Vicar of Christ to receive and act upon Heaven's perspective of timing and appropriateness, for the solemn definition of the truth of Mary Co-Redemptrix, and her subsequent roles as Mediatrix of all graces and Advocate for humanity. May this yearlong celebration of the 150th anniversary of the Immaculate Conception lead to a greater acknowledgement and praise of her sublime fullness of grace and her historic and continuous coredemption in the hearts of the People of God, and for the salvation of all humanity.

John Paul II has taught us that "Mary's role as Co-redemptrix did not cease with the glorification of her Son."[94] And he has recently re-iterated the truths of the Immaculate Conception and Marian Coredemption in his February 11, 2004 message for the World Day of the Sick:

> The keystone of history lies here: with the Immaculate Conception of Mary began the great work of Redemption that was brought to fulfillment in the precious blood of Christ . . . At the foot of the Cross Mary, made Mother of humanity, suffers in silence, participating in her Son's suffering, ready to intercede so that every person may obtain salvation.[95]

---

[94] John Paul II, *L'Osservatore Romano*, English edition, March 11, 1985, p. 7.

[95] John Paul II, "Mary Gives the Answer to Suffering: Jesus," for the Twelfth World Day of the Sick, February 11, 2004, *L'Osservatore Romano*, English edition, January 21, 2004, p. 7.

THE CONTRIBUTORS

DR. ROBERT A. STACKPOLE, S.T.D.

A convert from the Anglican Church, Dr. Stackpole holds a B.A. in history from William's College, a Certificate in Theological Studies from the University of California at Berkeley, an M.A. in theology from Oxford, and an S.T.D. from the Angelicum. He is currently a professor of theology at Redeemer Pacific College in British Columbia, and has lectured at the Dominican House of Studies in Washington, D.C. and the Franciscan University of Steubenville, Ohio. He is the author of a work in Christology based on the spirituality of St. Faustina Kowalska, *Jesus, Mercy Incarnate* (Marian Press, 2000), as well as the editor of many books and the author of many articles in various journals. He also serves as the Director of the John Paul II Institute of Divine Mercy in Stockbridge, MA, an apostolate of the Congregation of Marians of the Immaculate Conception.

SR. M. TIMOTHY PROKES, F.S.E., PH.D.

A Franciscan Sister of the Eucharist, Sr. Prokes has taught and lectured at numerous Universities in the United States and Canada, including being a visiting scholar at Lonergan University College, Concordia University, Montreal, Quebec. She holds a B.A. and M.A. from Marquette University, and a Ph.D. from the University of St. Michael's College, Toronto, Ontario, Canada. She is also a professor of the Permanent Diaconate Program of the Archdiocese of Washington, D.C. Her books include *Toward a Theology of the Body* (Eerdmans, 1997) and *Mutuality: The Human Image of Trinitarian Love* (Paulist, 1993). She has also published scholarly articles in such journals as

Communio and *National Catholic Bioethics Quarterly*. She is currently a professor at the Notre Dame Graduate School of Christendom College in Alexandria, Virginia.

Fr. Peter Damian Maria Fehlner, F.I., S.T.D.

A Franciscan Friar of the Immaculate, Fr. Fehlner has taught at various schools in the United States and Italy for over 40 years. He is a specialist in Franciscan theology and Mariology and earned his S.T.D. from the Seraphicum with a dissertation on the Ecclesiology of St. Bonaventure. In addition to being the editor (1985-1989) of the Marian review *Miles Immaculatae*, a review founded by St. Maximilian Kolbe in 1939, Fr. Fehlner has also translated the work by St. Thomas Aquinas *On the Reasons for Our Faith*, and written various books and articles, many of which are available through the Academy of the Immaculate Press. He currently lives in Rome where he teaches and serves the apostolate of his community in spreading devotion and knowledge about Our Lady.

Dr. Mary Shivanandan, S.T.D.

One of the leading scholars in expounding John Paul II's theology of the body, Dr. Shivanandan has taught theological anthropology at the John Paul II Institute in India and Australia, and at the Franciscan Seminary in Singapore. She holds B.A. and M.A. degrees in classics from Newnham College, Cambridge, as well as S.T.L. and S.T.D. degrees from the John Paul II Institute for Studies on Marriage & Family. She has written many books, including a leading work in the study of John Paul II's thought, *Crossing the Threshold of Love: A New Vision of Marriage in the Light of John Paul II's Anthropology* (CUA Press, 1999). She has also written scholarly articles for such journals as *Diakonia*, *Logos*, *Fides Quaerens Intellectum*, *Linacre Quarterly*, *Anthropotes*, *National Catholic Bioethics Quarterly* and *Catholic Social Science Review*. She is currently a professor of theology at the John Paul II Institute for Studies on Marriage & Family at the Catholic University of America.

FR. DONALD H. CALLOWAY, M.I.C.

A convert to Catholicism, Fr. Calloway is a member of the Congregation of Marians of the Immaculate Conception. As well as being a frequent speaker at Marian conferences across North America, he holds a B.A. in philosophy and theology from the Franciscan University of Steubenville, Ohio, M.Div. and S.T.B. degrees from the Dominican House of Studies in Washington, D.C., and is currently pursuing an S.T.L. in Mariology from the International Marian Research Institute in Dayton, Ohio. His conversion testimony is available through St. Joseph Communications and has been published, in brief, in *Amazing Grace for the Catholic Heart* (Ascension Press, 2003). He is a frequent contributor to *Homiletic & Pastoral Review*. He is currently the Assistant Shrine Rector of the National Shrine of The Divine Mercy in Stockbridge, MA.

DR. MARK I. MIRAVALLE, S.T.D.

President of the International Catholic Movement, Vox Populi Mariae Mediatrici, Dr. Miravalle is one of the leading Mariologists in the world today, lecturing internationally on such themes as Mary's role as Co-Redemptrix, Mediatrix of All Graces, and Marian apparitions. He holds a B.A. from the University of San Francisco, and S.T.L. & S.T.D. degrees from the Angelicum. He is the author of many books, including *With Jesus: The Story of Mary Co-Redemptrix* (Queenship, 2003) and *Introduction to Mary: The Heart of Marian Doctrine and Devotion* (Queenship, 1993). In addition to being the editor of many books dealing with Mary's role as Co-Redemptrix, Dr. Miravalle is a frequent contributor to the *National Catholic Register* and *Fidelity Magazine*, and also has an entry in the *New Catholic Encyclopedia*. He is currently a professor of theology & Mariology at the Franciscan University of Steubenville, Ohio.